Leapin' Lizards

...and other leaps of faith!

by Becky Yates Spencer

Copyright © 1999
Becky Yates Spencer

All rights reserved. No portion of this book may be reproduced by any means whatsoever, except for brief quotations in reviews, without written permission from the author.

The family photograph is furnished and copied with permission from Creative Reflections Photography, Halstead, Kansas.

Back cover photograph provided by David Boman.

Library of Congress Card Catalog Number: 99-94957

All Scripture quotations are taken from the King James Version of the Bible.

ISBN: 0-7392-0290-1

Printed in the USA by

MORRIS PUBLISHING

3212 East Highway 30 • Kearney, NE 68847 • 1-800-650-7888

CONTENTS

ACKNOWLEDGEMENTS. v
1. LEAPIN' LIZARDS I. 1
2. LEAP OF FAITH 4
3. LEAPING FROM THE LEDGES 17
4. LEAPIN' LIZARDS II. 37
5. LEAPIN' LIZARDS III. 45
6. LEAPING FLAMES. 51
7. THE BABE LEAPED IN HER WOMB 58
8. TEN LORDS A-LEAPING. 70
9. GROWING IN LEAPS AND BOUNDS 76
10. YOU CAUSED MY HEART TO LEAP INTO
    MY THROAT. 88
11. WALKING, LEAPING, AND PRAISING GOD . . 91
12. LOVER'S LEAP 100
13. WALKING AND LEAPING AND CARRYING
    THE TORCH. 111
14. LEAPING THROUGH HOOPS 115
15. TO THE "LEAPS" OF THESE. 125
    BOOKING INFORMATION. 131

Clockwise from back top: Jeri, Ben, Nathan, Ashley, Justin, Becky, Anna, Sara, Polly, and Tracy in the middle!

ACKNOWLEDGEMENTS

This book could never have been written without the input of many people, and I want to take time to thank those who have given so generously to this project.

First, let me thank the many women who have listened as I've shared our adoption story at mother/daughter banquets, ladies' organizations, and churches across the Mid-west. Your encouragement and requests to put our adventure into print caused me to consider and pray until I believed I had clear direction from the Lord to pursue this venture. You have blessed me as you've welcomed my family into your hearts and lives with your attentive, sensitive responses to my sharing.

Next, I want to thank my mother, Pattie Yates Belden, and my dear friends, Donna Abla, David Case, and Robbie Petitfils, for praying and pouring over the manuscript, encouraging me to dig deeper. Your faithful editing and suggestions gave me the courage I needed to tell the whole story.

Also, my daughter Sara was helpful when I didn't know how to operate certain computer functions, and she assisted me by printing out the manuscript. Thank you, honey!

Of course, all eight of my children deserve special thanks for being willing to let me share our lives through the years. You've been so giving, wanting others to understand what it has meant to us to serve Jesus by opening our home and our hearts. Bless you for being transparent so others can be touched!

Finally, I want to thank my husband, Tracy. Words are not enough to convey my deep gratitude to you. Not only have you cared for the children so I could write and travel to share our story, but you have been a faithful partner in this adventure of obedience. Not many men would give like you have. Not many would stick it out. Not many would work as hard, give up personal pursuits, and serve so selflessly. You have made it possible for me to realize my dreams, yet when I've asked you what I can do so you can follow your own dreams, you've told me you're already doing what you want to do. I know you could accomplish other things, inventing the gadgets you think up or going back to school or spending some weekends hunting or fishing or painting your truck. Still, you give your all. You are my stability, a solid oak that weathers the storms in our lives, and I love you with all my heart. Thank you for being a real daddy to our children and for being my very best friend. This book is lovingly dedicated to you.

1. LEAPIN' LIZARDS I

The only person I know to have used the phrase "Leapin' Lizards" is the fictitious red-headed "li'l orphant" girl we all know as Annie. I have vague recollections of reading the comic strip when I was a young girl, but the 1985 movie made her well-known to an entire generation of baby-busters. Whenever she was amazed about something, excited, or overcome, the enchanting child would exclaim, "Leapin' lizards!" and we all looked on, sharing her awe at a world much greater than the one she had known at the orphanage.

Daddy Warbucks, the billionaire who eventually loved Annie and adopted her, was our hero. He was bigger-than-life, able to right the world with a snarl and a command, but he was putty in Annie's hand, which endeared him to us. How true that a needy child can cut through our tough exteriors and get our undivided attention!

Children who are hurting have always demanded my attention, so it's no surprise that God led my husband, Tracy, and I on a journey that included adoption. In fact, when I see a troubled child, my *first* inclination is to take him or her home with me! I'd take them in like some people care for pets that have been left in the countryside--if Tracy didn't stop me! My interest most certainly stems from a difficult childhood, growing up with an alcoholic father. Knowing firsthand what it feels like to cry out for stability and a sense of order, my heart naturally pulls towards needy children.

Moving from caring to doing was an adventure, though! In the spring of 1990, I was already busy serving God. In addition to being a wife and rearing three children, I was teaching elementary music and junior high English at Central Christian School in Hutchinson, Kansas. Having already put in many hours previously teaching adult Sunday school, leading worship at church, and helping sponsor youth group, I felt my plate was full enough and I needed a break from working with children outside of school.

Years earlier, in the summer of 1983, two teenaged sisters, Angie and LeAnn, had come to live with us for three years, so we'd already gotten our feet wet with taking in children. Still, we weren't really looking for additional service in that department.

During a chapel service at Central Christian, however, a video grabbed my attention--and my heart. The Scripture reading was from Matthew 25, where Jesus separated the sheep from the goats. The only difference between the two was their actions! I was stunned! No matter how many times I re-read the passage, teaching Sunday school and leading worship and teaching in a Christian school weren't listed there! No, the kinds of things the sheep did were feeding the hungry, giving drink to the thirsty, inviting in strangers, clothing the naked, looking after the sick, and visiting prisoners. I was shaken as the Holy Spirit began to break up the hard soil of my heart; I cried throughout the rest of chapel and off and on all day. Thankfully, my students were compassionate and didn't intrude, because I couldn't have voiced what I was feeling.

By the time I arrived home from school with Sara, Nathan, and Ben, our 11-, 8-, and 5 year olds, respectively, it was clear I was simply going through the motions of my chores at home. Mechanically making dinner when Tracy arrived home from work, I was still crying openly, and I fell into his arms immediately. Naturally, he was concerned, but I put him off until we had finished dinner and the dishes were out of the way so we could talk without interruption.

As I shared the Scripture from Matthew with him, Tracy, too, was touched deeply. We began to seek the Lord together, and it was clear to us that He was asking something of us much bigger than anything we had ever ventured before. We read the passage from Matthew several times that evening while we prayed and wept before God, asking Him for direction as to what He would have us do. Before the evening was done, we were convinced that the Lord wanted us to take in strangers, and that they would be small ones! We knew He was calling us to adopt. "Leapin' Lizards!"

2. LEAP OF FAITH

Now, all the birth order teachings say that if you adopt, the new family member should be younger than your youngest child. This is supposed to prevent the "pecking order" that children seem to experience, and the advice is designed to ensure that the previously existing child doesn't feel replaced or demoted in any way. We already had one girl and two boys, so it made sense to begin praying that the Lord would lead us to a little girl, younger than Ben-- and preferably potty-trained!

I evaluated our family and what I believed we had to offer. Especially looking at the children, I wanted to be sure we got a good "fit." Sara was responsible with a capital "R." She was compliant and a willing helper, just waiting to help "mother" whomever God sent our way. Nathan was easy-going, yet spiritually alert. He was deeply drawn to the Lord and loved to worship, especially singing. I knew he would be a warrior in whatever spiritual battles we faced. Ben's humorous approach to life was already one of the highlights of our days, so I knew he would make home fun for our new little one and would help keep our spirits up when needed.

Naturally, I also looked at what Tracy and I had to offer, and I was sure Ward and June Cleaver from "Leave It to Beaver" had nothing on us. I was confident we would be able to love a child with the love of the Lord, sure our faith would move mountains in a needy child's life, and I was anxious to get the ball rolling.

I began calling adoption agencies all over Kansas, excited that we were embarking on what we knew the Lord had called us to do. It didn't take long for my enthusiasm to drain, however. One by one, I learned that each adoption agency either didn't have children in the age-group we were seeking, or they charged over $30,000 to complete the adoption. I moved to the international arena, only to learn that adopting a child from Romania would be equally expensive--or more so. I contacted over thirty agencies, but the answer was always the same: we couldn't afford their services.

I must admit that I began to be more than a little irritated--mostly with the system, which whined about the need for adoptive parents, then made it almost impossible for the average person to respond to the need. I have to confess that I was also a little bit irritated with the Lord. I questioned, "Lord, if You really want us to do this, why aren't You making a way?" I began to entertain doubts in the back of my mind, uncertain where else I could look for a child. Time was ticking away. One and a half years passed while we prayed and waited for God to send us the little girl He wanted us to adopt.

One source Tracy and I had dismissed was Social and Rehabilitative Services (SRS), because they informed us they wouldn't have a little girl in the age-range we were looking for. When a child is three to five years old, SRS was usually still trying to work with the child's birth family to provide training and parenting skills necessary to allow the family unit to remain intact or be reunited. When we were discouraged enough to quit looking, my friend Connie Montgomery told me about an agency in Pueblo, Colorado. Loving Homes was a Christian adoption agency that worked with SRS to find Christian homes for children in the system who wouldn't be able to reunite with their families. The fees were relatively low; for about $500 - $800, parents and children could be matched and begin a life together. Tracy and I were encouraged and made the call to Loving Homes. The social worker there thought they could find us a little girl, and we were ecstatic as we began filling out stacks of paperwork to mail to them! We had our fingerprints "done" at the local police station for the required background check and spent about six hours filling out the first of the forms necessary to begin the adoption process.

Meanwhile, SRS in Hutchinson sent us a letter informing us of the foster/adoptive parenting classes they were offering, called MAPP training. Only the Lord knows how He was able to get our attention to consider these classes, since we were convinced that SRS wouldn't be able to find us a daughter! Somehow God got through, though, and regardless of our reservations, we decided that we'd go to the first class just to see what it was like. Tracy and I felt sure the teaching would be on the humanistic side of things as far as world-view goes, thereby conflicting with our Christian beliefs. We set aside our paperwork for Loving Homes, sure that we'd come back to it and mail it within a week or two.

Well, the first class was fantastic! Not only was it completely unoffensive to our faith, but the training was excellent, helping equip parents with the skills needed to minister to the various loss, attachment, and grief issues children in foster or adoptive care invariably face. Tracy and I decided to finish the ten week course that included thirty hours of training.

Only two weeks into the training, our community was hit with a tragedy. On September 14, 1991, during the Kansas State Fair, Debra, mother of four children, was reported missing. The newspapers gave a detailed account of the search for her, and her children were pictured on the front page with their father. Their faces were riveting--forlorn and hopeless. At the Christian school, every time we took prayer requests, these children were at the top of the list. At home, we prayed, too, that Debra would be found, but as the days passed without any news, we weren't holding out much hope. Sure enough, two weeks after her disappearance, her body was discovered and her husband, Eddie, was arrested for her murder.

Eddie was known for his excessive drinking. In fact, the children had called the police on many occasions previous to Debra's death; while intoxicated, he would get into physical fights with Debra, terrifying the children and leaving them no choice but to call for help in order to protect their mother.

The children had much more than their father's drinking to contend with. As is often the case with women in abusive relationships, Debra had "shut down" in many areas. She was barely coping with just getting through each day, and she had a bad back on top of the emotional strain. Nurturing activities like feeding the family, doing the laundry, or keeping the house clean were sometimes overwhelming. Polly had become a second mother to her younger siblings, and she did her best to make sure they ate and got ready for school. Many animals, such as ducks and pigs, shared their trailor located north of Hutchinson, Kansas.

Eddie was cruel to the children when on a drunken binge, especially to his daughter Jeri. He called her stupid and made fun of her. Justin remembered his father locking Jeri in the shed. One aunt related the story that Eddie would also handcuff the children to their Wonder Horse. Polly shared the account of several fires being started in the fields near their trailer, with the wind blowing the fires towards it. She and her sisters and brother were home when these fires occurred, and her father was in the fields each time. Although there was never enough evidence to convict Eddie of arson, Polly believed with all her heart that her father had set the fires in an attempt to burn the children in their trailer. Whether he was guilty of an attempt on their lives or not was not relevant to Polly's *belief* that he had, nor the fear she lived with for the safety of her mother and siblings whom she felt responsible to care for.

All of the extended family agreed that when Eddie was sober, he was a loving father. He adored his son, Justin, and took the boy with him whenever he could. He loved to spend time with all the children, and often took them with him on trips into town. Unfortunately, though, those trips frequently ended up at the liquor store. The children remember being forced to take drinks of beer, and sometimes they would smash all of Eddie's full beer bottles in an effort to make him stop drinking. There was no doubt in their minds where the meanness came from, and they wanted it to end.

They couldn't have understood at their tender ages that many other factors entered into the make-up of their father's personality. Eddie had certainly had a rough life, beginning with his parents' divorce when he was a small child. At the age of nine, his mother took him to visit his father; she never came back for him. The rejection he experienced certainly plagued him and was a force that partially shaped the man he eventually became. He spent the rest of his childhood with his father and step-mother, a godly woman who did her best to influence Eddie for good.

As a teenager, though, Eddie dropped out of high school and ended up joining the armed forces, serving our country in Viet Nam. We will probably never know how much influence that experience had on his behaviors. We know that a time comes in every person's life when he must take responsibility for his own choices instead of blaming parents, circumstances, or the past; still, it is easy to see that Eddie had many strikes against him from early on.

Debra had accepted Christ as her Savior about a year-and-a-half before her murder, and she had been faithfully taking the children to church. She longed for a different life for her family and had warned Eddie that she wanted the drinking to stop, but he was not interested in seeking help for himself. In fact, he had even bragged to a liquor store clerk that he planned to kill Debra because she was giving him a hard time about his drinking. Bravely, Debra had checked on information about a shelter in Wichita where she and the children could have a reprieve from Eddie's foul alcohol-induced moods and abuse, but there was a waiting list to get in. How I cried when I learned that just days after her death, the awaited letter arrived saying that there was an opening at the shelter for Debra and the children!

The evening of Debra's disappearance, Eddie had been drinking again. Debra had stayed up late playing Nintendo, one of her favorite pastimes. Polly and Justin said that they knew something was amiss the next morning, because Debra had left the game and lights on. Jeri had heard her father's truck start up during the night, so she got up and looked out her bedroom window. She saw her mother and father both in the truck as he pulled out. Remaining perched at the window the entire time of her parents' absence, she knew her father had done something terrible when she saw him return alone.

Eddie had taken Debra to Medora bridge, not far from their trailer, and had held her face in the sand until she suffocated. He dumped her into the water and left her there, pretending later that she had disappeared in the night. He went to the neighboring houses to inquire whether anyone had seen or heard from her. The children remained alone in their pain, not breaking the unspoken code of loyalty and silence, though they all knew deep down that their father was guilty of taking their mother's life.

The four children were split up after their father's arrest. They spent a few days with their paternal grandparents, then Polly went to her Aunt Karen's house, her mother's half-sister. Jeri was with her Aunt Kristy, her mother's sister. Ashley ended up staying with friends of the family in Medora, while Justin was with his Aunt Jackie, another half-sister to his mother.

The paternal grandmother was praying for a Christian home for the children--one where they could be together and have some stability. She and the children's grandfather were already raising one of their grandchildren, and at their ages, didn't feel starting again with four little ones was the best plan.

She asked Pastor Wayne and Lorri Johnson, who pastor Medora Community Bible Church near Hutchinson, to consider taking the children.

Well, it so happened that Wayne and Lorri also taught at Central Christian. At lunch one day early in October, Lorri confided in me that she and Wayne didn't feel the Lord was leading them to take the children. That made sense; they hadn't been married long, and they had no children yet. In passing, I reminded Lorri that Tracy and I were praying about adopting and maybe we could take the children. When I got home that evening, I mentioned my conversation with Lorri to Tracy and the children, but none of us gave it a lot of thought.

Much to my surprise, the next morning at school, Lorri asked me what we had decided--the grandma wanted to know! I couldn't believe things were suddenly moving so quickly! Distracted all day at school, I couldn't wait to get home and ask Tracy what he thought! He and I and our children talked about the children's needs all through dinner that evening.

The more we talked, the more obvious it became that it just didn't make good sense for us to take the children. For one thing, we were renting a house that was plenty big for that many people, but it was for sale--and way out of our price range. We knew that when the owners got serious about selling, we'd be looking for other lodging. We owned a home in a nearby community, but it was too small for nine people. We also drove a six-passenger car, and really didn't have the funds to purchase a van (or small bus!) for a larger family. Just as importantly, I *hated* to cook! I knew we wouldn't be able to afford trips even to McDonald's with that many children! The funny thing was, the more we talked about why it didn't make sense to take the children, the more we wanted them!

I knew Tracy would need time to think and pray, so I left him alone--for an hour! He sorts through issues inwardly, but I need verbalization, and lots of it! After the sixty minute interlude, I tracked him down in our bedroom and asked him what he thought. He cocked his head to one side and pulled on his beard, deep in thought, then asked me to get his Bible. I always know good things are coming when he says that! Tracy opened the pages to the passage of Scripture he had read that very morning, Mark 9:36-37: "And he [Jesus] took a little child and set him in the midst of [the Twelve]: and when he had taken him in his arms, he said unto them, 'Whosoever shall receive one of such children in my name receiveth me; and whosoever shall receive me, receiveth not me, but him that sent me.'" Tears brimming from my eyes, I quietly asked Tracy if that was a "yes." He replied that if the children needed us, he thought we should be there for them.

We called Sara, Nathan, and Ben in to tell them our decision to be available if it worked out, and they were thrilled! We discussed the fact that it might not be easy, but that we'd actually be inviting Jesus into our home and we'd be ministering to Him, since however we treated the children would be how we were really treating Him!

Now, just a side-note. What if Tracy hadn't been in the habit of reading his Bible each day? I believe the Lord still could have gotten through to us, but how much more confident we were that He had spoken to us through the very place where Tracy "happened" to be reading, anyway! We don't believe in coincidence--only God-incidents! Many times since then, when doubts have begun to assail, we've been able to go back to this verse for reassurance that we're following God's plan for us. Tracy and I don't read our Bibles *every* day, but that's the goal and plan. It isn't a legalistic activity that we think determines our favor with God or proves how righteous we are; instead, it's an invaluable tool that helps keep us on track--and we need all the help we can get!

I went back to school the next morning and reported to Lorri that if it worked out legally, we'd take the children. The next day, Friday, I decided to call SRS. At that point, the agency didn't even have the case, but the social worker wrote down our names just in case it crossed her desk. God's timing is amazing; the following Monday, Judge Patty Macke-Dick awarded us custody of the children!

The plan was to foster parent the children while waiting to see what their father's fate would be. If he were found guilty, his parental rights would be severed and the children would be available for adoption. We didn't relish the idea of foster parenting, knowing we would come to love the children, but that we might have to give them up. We weren't sure how we'd support such a large family, either. Tracy and I--and our birth children--were completely convinced that God was leading us, though, so we took the leap of faith.

We had only one introductory meeting with the children and the various family members they were staying with. I was nervous, wanting to find ways to put the children--and myself--at ease. My friend Tammy Bussard (Dudley now) was a friend of the children's Aunt Kathy, and she knew that Justin liked horses. I prepared by going to the library earlier and checking out the largest horse picture book I could find. I also made rice crispie treats to share in order to have something to do with our hands while we visited--and so nobody would feel too pressured to talk. The book was a big hit with Justin, and he climbed up into my lap for a few minutes to see the pictures. Ashley shyly sat on my lap awhile, too. Polly and Jeri didn't have much to say to us, but naturally, the children's family members had a few questions for us. All too quickly, the meeting was over, and we knew the next time we saw these children, they would be moving in!

On Saturday, October 26th, 1991, the children came to live with us. Polly was twelve years old, Jeri was ten, Ashley was six, and Justin was three. They were sandwiched in age with our birth children, who were then twelve, nine, and six. What an adventure began that day! All I can say is, God obviously never read *The Birth Order Book!*

3. LEAPING FROM THE LEDGES

I would be amiss if I pretended that the children moved in, we all loved each other on sight, and our family lived happily ever after! Those kinds of fairy tales only exist in juvenile fiction. In fact, that first weekend we had the children, I was completely overwhelmed! We were strangers, trying to get settled in together while getting to know each other, hoping it was going to be a very long-term relationship. That experience gave me some inkling what brides and grooms experience in marriages where the parents have arranged the wedding without the parties ever meeting!

We weren't sure exactly how to prepare for the children's arrival; usually people have nearly nine months to get ready, and they usually get kids one at a time! Besides locating a nine passenger vehicle, we also needed to arrange for beds, bedding, and closet and dresser space. We couldn't have done it without the help of some very special people. Dwane and Betty Parker gave us two sets of brand new bunkbeds and several sets of sheets and blankets. They were so involved, making the transition easier for all of us. A furniture store south of Hutchinson also helped by donating the four mattresses for the beds.

I had arranged for the kids to arrive one hour apart, so that it wouldn't be quite as chaotic as if they all descended at the same time. It didn't end up working that way, and I can't quite remember why, but they showed up relatively closely together. I was quickly learning that my "need" for organization was going to go out the window!

The first few minutes are a blur to me. I know I was trying to show each child which bedroom belonged to him or her and to re-introduce all of the family. The social worker was trying to finish paperwork and the phone was ringing a lot. Emotions were running high as the kids' relatives were saying their goodbyes. I can only imagine how difficult it was for them to leave their precious little ones in the care of strangers!

The first task was getting clothing needs met for the children. SRS had given us $250 for each child for clothing, and it all had to be spent that first weekend. I wanted to sort through the kids' belongings so I could determine what they needed. As they came in with their sacks and boxes of clothes and toys, I had their relatives place everything in the seldom-used dining room. Much to my horror, as I began looking through the assortment, cockroaches started crawling out onto my carpet! I thought surely there would be only a few, and I didn't want to make the kids feel badly, so I tried to unobtrusively kill each bug I saw while making an effort to continue sorting.

Most of the clothes were not in good repair, or they were stained. Still, my drive to be thorough pushed me on, and I kept going through things, one child at a time by my side to tell me which were their favorites. I'd learned in my parenting class that you must not throw out anything that could have sentimental value, so I had to take care to consider the feelings of each child. Finally, I couldn't take any more and decided we'd put their things in the garage to sort through when we had become better adjusted.

Our shopping trips on that first Saturday and Sunday were bizarre! Not only was I ignorant of what the children needed, but I didn't know their sizes nor taste in clothing. I wanted them to feel free to choose things they would really like, so we took a long time looking around and trying on outfits. Naturally, since we didn't know each other, there were some awkward moments. These kids weren't used to being able to buy so many new things at once, and frankly, neither was I. I was afraid we'd forget something vitally important, but the money would already be spent. If you ever take in foster children, trust me-- just get jeans, shirts, something to wear to Sunday school, underwear, jammies, and either a coat or a swimsuit! It's okay if you later discover they already had an item and it's been duplicated! We finally decided on enough to get them by, and we headed home to begin putting their belongings in their new bedrooms.

The real challenge began when we began to actually situate the children in their rooms. Sara and Polly shared a room. Sara was convinced she was finally getting a sister who would be her best friend.

She was one of only two granddaughters in our family, and the other one was six years younger than she, so she thought it was ideal that Polly was only three months her junior. Sara envisioned the two of them staying up at night sharing secrets, like which boy they had a crush on or what funny thing had happened in class that day. Polly, on the other hand, was extremely withdrawn and uncommunicative. She was not at all outgoing and had experienced great loss; for her, this was no slumber party. Her entire life was being turned upside down, and I'm sure she was scared to death. She knew intuitively that her role with the children was going to change, and that brought a stress all its own. She had no intention of sharing anything, not even surface events. This was *not* going to be a bosom buddy situation!

Jeri came to us with special needs beyond those of losing her parents. It didn't take long for us to see we had a real challenge on our hands. Those first few evenings, after dinner and dishes were done, I would announce that it was time to do homework. Jeri would immediately begin screaming--yes, screaming, not yelling! She didn't want to do her homework! We first tried letting her join the rest of the family to study, but nobody could even think with her in the room; regretfully, I banned her to her bedroom to do her work. Even then, she would come into the hall upstairs, hang over the bannister, and continue screaming, pausing occasionally to look over the stairs to see if anybody was listening! It was torture for everyone, but we knew she had to learn to take instruction and do the required school work. Jeri had wide mood swings, either cheerfully chatting non-stop about every detail of her day or grousing at the rest of us because she was frustrated with the world.

Jeri was sharing a room with Ashley. At first, I really worried about Ashley, because she didn't do anything wrong! She was the most perfect child I'd ever met. Her obedience wasn't healthy, though. I think she felt like she'd entered a fairy land world, and she wanted to be sure she didn't do something that would cause us to send her away. We wouldn't have done that, but she didn't know it at the time, and her insecurity wouldn't let her relax even for a minute! She must have been inwardly stressed, timidly tiptoeing around on imaginary eggshells existing only in her own mind.

Little Justin was in a room with Ben and Nathan, with the two younger boys enjoying bunk beds and Nathan on a twin bed of his own. Justin wasn't convinced it was necessary to obey these new strangers he'd had thrust into his life! We can laugh now, but the first day he came to live with us was far from funny at the time! He had taken a bracelet that belonged to Ashley, and she was trying to get him to return it. He wouldn't cooperate with her, so I stopped in to help. When he disregarded my request to give it back to her, I simply picked him up to get on eye level with him, but he went berserk! He began hitting and kicking and screaming, "I want down! I want Sissy (meaning Polly)!"

Believe me, I wanted to put him down, because I was on the receiving end of his little cowboy boots! Intuitively, though, I knew I needed to "win" this confrontation, so I held on and kept repeating, "Justin, I want to put you down. I want to give you to Sissy, too, but in our house, the children do what the parents say." He continued to kick and hit and scream--for forty-five minutes! I'd never prayed so hard in my life! I wasn't sure I was doing the right thing, but I *so* wanted to help him realize there was a higher authority that had his good in mind! Finally, he agreed to return the bracelet, so I tenderly lowered his feet to the carpet, at which time he promptly threw the bracelet on the floor! We went another thirty minutes before he agreed to give it back to Ashley nicely!

Justin wasn't used to taking naps, either, and I knew he'd have to lie down at day care while I taught school. I told him if he'd just stay in the bed for twenty minutes, he wouldn't even have to sleep. I set the kitchen timer and we all rejoiced when he remained horizontal for the full time! He had to sit in time out a few times for other offenses, but within three days, he really had come to understand the ground rules in his new home.

There were so many other issues those first few days. The children came with severe cases of head lice. We learned the first night that three of the children wet the bed almost every night, meaning additional laundry and giving lots of reassurance so they weren't humiliated or embarrassed. We were trying to adjust and gently ease them into our way of family life. We still had to do the regular things like preparing and eating meals, cleaning the house, trying to keep up with the insurmountable mounds of laundry, nightly routines of bathing, and so on. I had papers to grade and lesson plans to go over, along with lectures and concerts to prepare since I was teaching full-time.

Mealtime alone was a lot for me to tackle. I already disliked culinary endeavors, but being a somewhat picky eater myself, I wanted to be sure the kids had food they liked, especially for the first few meals. I had to adjust quantities, and it took awhile to find the right measurements of seasonings. We had to add a leaf to the kitchen table, making us terribly cramped, but the dining room was far too fancy for us.

I had to redefine the word *clean*. Reminding myself that the new kids probably thought their rooms *were* clean compared to what they were used to, I lowered my standards in order to keep the peace. Although I hated to change my expectations, I knew that the children would not be able to tolerate being nagged incessantly about the way they did their chores. It was more important that they feel welcomed and accepted and successful in their new environment.

The house we were renting came already

furnished, including lovely glassware displayed in cabinets, and I was worried that we'd ruin something, so it was difficult to relax. I wanted the kids to feel completely at home as soon as possible, but since the home wasn't ours, there was added stress.

    At about 9:00 both of those first two nights we had the children, I made my way into the bathroom, closed the door, and wailed! We're not talking here about shedding a few tears; we're talking full-blown sobs, complete with the wet face, red nose, and all. The Scripture in Romans 8 that says the Spirit prays for us with groanings that cannot be uttered took on new meaning for me! I didn't have the time nor the energy to evaluate how things were going; I just needed the Lord's touch to survive each hour of each day!

    As the weeks passed, we gradually adjusted. Still, there were many issues to face. Polly still *wouldn't* respond to people, and even when asked a question, she barely grunted a response. She still felt responsible for her siblings, and hardly knew what to do when Tracy and I began to parent them. She knew being with us was good for the children, so she tolerated the situation, but it was still hard for her to see the two younger children warming to us so quickly. Many nights she cried herself to sleep, thinking nobody could hear her muffled sobs. It was so hard for her--and for Jeri--to accept our love as parents, much less to return it as our children.

    Just a few weeks after coming to live with us,

I spoke with Polly about her responses to people, or the lack thereof! I let her know that I understood life had been hard for her, and that it was only normal to be distrustful of people and to want to be left alone. Still, I made it clear that being rude to others was absolutely not acceptable. She was expected to answer when spoken to, shake an outstretched hand, and respond to those who reached out to her. She was not happy with this direction, but I didn't back down.

One major step for her during those early weeks was asking to transfer to Central Christian the end of first semester. The other children were all already attending Central, but we'd given Polly the choice of staying at her former school or joining the rest of us. There had been an almost unbearable amount of change in her life without switching schools on top of that, but we knew she would be battling the preconceived image other kids at her previous school had about her. The teachers and students at Central had been completely accepting of the other children; I think it spoke to Polly's heart, too. Transferring was her way of letting us know she wanted to be connected to the rest of us. She was warmly received, as I knew she would be, and she began to blossom as she established a new identity.

Jeri slowly made progress, but school was hard for her. With a learning disability, it took lots of extra effort, but after six months of perseverance on our part *and* hers, she realized that we weren't going to back down about studies. Every school night would involve study time. She finally gave up her tirades. I'm not sure that the studying improved much at that time, but at least the rest of us could read or review in peace.

Although extremely extroverted and a social butterfly, Jeri wasn't skilled in reading other people's boundaries, which made for some rocky relationships. At home, she exhibited lots of passive aggressive behavior. When I read a book about it, I finally knew what name to give the blocked pathways, taking extended time to tell a simple story, purposely irritating others, and so much more. People who are terribly angry, but don't feel they can express their anger, often show it in more subtle and destructive ways such as those I've mentioned.

We learned more about how Jeri was affected by the mistreatment she suffered in her home of origin. We may never know the extent of her abuse, but for some reason, she received more of it than the other children. This complicated her need for acceptance and the way she looked for it. Although she wanted attention and longed to be loved, the only thing that felt "normal" to her was to have people upset with her. It seemed easier to her to gain the attention she craved by misbehaving than through more age-appropriate behaviors. Jeri acted out her abusive treatment by turning it on the other children. It was all we could do to keep up, knowing she needed almost continual supervision.

Shy, sweet, and sensitive, Ashley quickly became a favorite at school with classmates and teachers alike because of her eagerness to please. Still, insecurity is not a good motivation for compliance, and I worried that she'd become a life-long people pleaser. Many hours were spent in prayer for this precious little one who seemed to need extra protection from the world.

Justin was well-behaved for the most part, but he was often lost in the shuffle. Being younger, he went to bed earlier than the other children, so I didn't have much time with him in the evenings. I feared that his needs were far from being met, but didn't know how to stretch myself any further than I already was being stretched.

I knew that parenting was a challenge even under the best of circumstances, much less with the special needs our children faced. Our birth kids' needs were compounded during this adjustment time when we simply were not available to them like we used to be. We were learning daily that even when God has called you to a task or ministry, this doesn't mean it will all be smooth sailing! There's a reason people talk about the "work" of the ministry!

Six months after the children came, we learned that our landlords wanted us to move so they could get serious about selling the house. We looked and looked for a house that was big enough for us, yet still in our budget. Our real estate agent, Linda Stringer, was an angel. She showed us everything she could find--and then some! Nothing was right for us, though, and our time was running out. There were probably days when Linda thought we were too picky, but she never showed it if she did! I simply couldn't settle for a house that would not meet our needs. I wanted space! We needed a large living room and dining room where we would all fit at the same time, because family was of the utmost importance.

We finally had to move in with my parents. They lived in a two bedroom duplex with only one-and-a-half bathrooms! There were eleven of us, and you'd think it would have been horrendous. It *was* challenging because of the cramped quarters, but we found out again that the Lord knows what He's doing. The first weekend at the folks', I had to be gone for a trip with my eighth graders. That week was also the kids' first time to go through what would have been their mother's birthday without her. It was also Jeri's first birthday without her mom. On top of that, their dad's trial took place that week! Mama was so good; she cooked all the meals. (Yes! You already know I don't like that part of being the mom!) She held little ones and comforted them. She provided stability and helped us tremendously as we attempted to meet the needs of our large family. Daddy was good to take the boys fishing and to be a ready listener for all of us. They were such a help to us, but it was still stressful; you just can't make such a small place really workable for that many people for too long!

We were with Mom and Dad for three-and-a-half months, at which time we moved into our Buhler house. The first time Linda took us to see it, I knew as soon as we entered the front door that it was the right one--before even seeing the whole house. The peace of God came over me, and I knew we were home. Still, change is always stressful, and it took weeks for us to get settled.

A local church had helped us financially and so had our friends, Hulse and Carol Wagner, so we were able to not only purchase the home, but do some work on it, too.

We frantically painted walls and kitchen cupboards. We wall-papered--and stayed married! Ha! We sanded and refinished wood floors. In two-and-a-half weeks, we had the house ready to move into. What bonding took place as we worked together on a house that *all* of us had chosen together!

My time was *too* stretched. I loved teaching, but it was almost more than I could do to care for my family and my students. I have to admit that Tracy is the one who suffered the most for my busy-ness. I also lost contact with any local friendships I was trying to develop. Suddenly, there just wasn't time to devote to relationships other than the children God had placed in my life. Even my quiet time alone with Jesus began to suffer. Prayer and Bible study became luxuries instead of daily bread to me, and I missed the intimacy I'd known with the Lord. He was still near, but I wasn't tapping into His presence like I wanted to. I was lonely.

Tracy's schedule was full, too, because even when he wasn't working overtime trying to provide for us, he was working on our vehicles. We'd been able to find an old van to seat the nine of us, but it continually needed repairs. We didn't have the funds to hire any help, nor to go out with others--or even each other very often. We were losing contact quickly and didn't know what to do about it. The days passed into weeks and months, and we didn't really realize how far we were drifting from one another.

Other things were difficult, too. Since the adopted children lost their mother during the Kansas State Fair, we found it was a difficult time of year at our house. Tracy's father also died during the fair, in September, 1992, one year after Debra's death.

One of the things Polly *did* open up about was the game she and her mom would play every year at the fair. Usually so private, Polly told and retold that memory, with her misty eyes looking far away to the mother she loved and missed. She couldn't quite let herself cry in front of us, because it was too painful to let the memories begin in the light of day. This one little event was almost all she would allow herself.

Jeri didn't reminisce, at least not outwardly. Her feelings caused her to become irritable for most of the month of September. Ashley, never one to challenge authority, still grew silent and depressed during that time of year. Even Justin, who couldn't have possibly known the dates, still reacted to the anniversary of his mother's death by misbehaving or being uncooperative in day care or class. So many times I felt like I was in over my head when it came to knowing how to help with the loss and attachment issues the children faced. They received two-and-a-half years of therapy, but it seemed only time and life experiences with God's help could really begin to bring healing.

Another difficulty we encountered was the long wait for the adoption. Eddie had appealed his first conviction, where he had received the "hard 40," meaning he wouldn't be eligible for parole for forty years. Finally, in the spring of 1994, his legal proceedings were over and he received a life sentence, eligible for parole in fifteen years. We knew that if he were to be released from prison at that time, Justin, the youngest of the children, would be eighteen years old, so I breathed a sigh of relief. It would have been much harder to deal with if he had received a sentence that would have given him the opportunity for face-to-face contact with the children before they reached adulthood.

After Eddie's trial and appeal came the long wait for SRS to complete their paperwork, since parental rights of the birth father were finally severed. By November, 1994, we were extremely tired of waiting. My birthday was the 18th, and Ashley made me a lovely card. On the back she had written that she hoped for my birthday SRS would say we got to keep the children. I was so touched and hurt for her--and hopping mad that it was taking so long! We adults knew the adoption would go through, but the poor children weren't sure of anything! Ashley in particular struggled with needing to have it all settled legally--she needed assurance that nobody could ever take her away from us!

I called SRS the next day and read the birthday card Ashley had given to me to our social worker. I let her know I expected things to move along rapidly from that point on, and she complied. On February 17th, 1995, the children legally became Spencers!

When we first got the children, I'd pictured the eventual day of our adoption through rose-colored glasses. I imagined the joy each child would experience and how close we would be as a family. After the three-and-a-half years of waiting, certainly we had grown closer to each other, but there was also much pain present. Polly and Jeri were struggling; they wanted us to adopt them, but to change their names almost felt to them like a rejection of their birth family. Their loyalties were being torn, and I was challenged to let them know how privileged I felt to be their adoptive mother, while at the same time giving them space and "permission" to grieve. Tracy and I let them know we would be happy for them to keep their birth names as part of their names, so they added Spencer to the tail end of their existing names. Ashley and Justin chose to drop their former names.

We made a day of the adoption, even though we

knew it was bitter-sweet. Tracy and I took all seven of the children out of school; we spent the day attending the court hearing and signing of legal documents together; having our picture taken with Judge Patty Macke-Dick and our attorney, Ken Pierce; eating lunch out with members of my family; renting a room at a hotel so we could swim, play games, and order food; and finally attending a Bryan Duncan concert in Wichita! I'd spoken with the sponsor of the concert, and they announced our adoption during intermission--it was so much fun! We still celebrate February 17th as a special day, in addition to October 26th every year, which is the day the children came to live with us. Any excuse for a party!

Life isn't always a party, though. Our birth children have had to cope with the loss of time with us. Realistically, no matter how hard we've tried to be sure everyone gets attention, we just can't stretch far enough. Time flies by, and we realize months and years have passed, and the older children are starting to leave home; we don't feel we've had enough input individually with them.

We probably never feel like we've had enough time with those we love. I lost my own father May 30th, 1998. It's the hardest thing I've experienced so far. Daddy had quit drinking for the most part when I was in junior high school. We had developed a precious relationship; in fact, he was one of my best friends. He seemed to understand me better that anyone else did; we were so much alike!

In the summer of 1995, we learned Daddy was ill with leukemia, so over three years, we tried to prepare ourselves to deal with the last stages of his disease. We didn't realize he'd suffered a heart attack in May of 1998 until the end of the month. He had surgery for a blocked artery, and passed away the evening of the surgery. He would have wanted every last precious moment with us, even if it meant more pain, but I had to be glad for him that he didn't have to suffer with the final ravaging stage of the leukemia.

Still, losing Daddy was almost too much for me, along with the other stress I was carrying; I didn't slip into depression--I slammed into it! I could barely get out of bed in the mornings, and I found the daily tasks of preparing meals and keeping up with the laundry were almost too much to bear. Two of our teenagers were seriously rebelling during this time. Our van had broken down again, and our car soon followed suit. Tracy was constantly consumed with trying to provide reliable transportation.

Children in rebellion, stresses and cares of this life, facing our own losses--along with the crises in identity that accompany those adjustments--all have tested my limits. Being a person of faith doesn't mean being immune to the hardships of life. Like so many of my brothers and sisters in Christ who are facing the realities of being rescuers and needing to redefine some healthy boundaries, I've felt pushed right to the edge of the ledge. I've wondered how to balance the

Scriptures that say that the Lord won't give us more than we can bear, that we should bear one another's burdens, and that each of us should carry his own load! Questions about how much of my load is truly the one the Lord has given me come to mind. Have I taken on some that aren't mine to carry? Is there someone who is supposed to be sharing the load, but they aren't sensitive to the Lord's leading--or have I been too proud to admit I have a need? My closest friends all live away from us and time doesn't seem to allow for developing new relationships of depth; are we meant to go through life alone? While searching for the answers, I have to admit that I've been occasionally tempted to take a leap.

God has used my strong husband to help keep me from careening off the edge. My long distance telephone has been a life line as I call my dear friends Liz and Robbie for comfort and prayer. Having friends from years ago come back into our lives has also been a lifesaver. I'd lost contact with Diann for several years, but her daughter Rachelle showed up on our door out of the clear blue--right when I needed Diann desperately. We were able to pick up right where we'd left off, and it felt so good to share my heart and hear hers, as well. Melody and Jason have faithfully loved Tracy and I through some of the roughest times of our lives. All of these people, along with my parents and brothers and sisters, have kept me sane by standing by me during dark days when it has seemed all hope was gone.

So I've made it through those scary times when I couldn't see past the pain. And now, *I* must take some steps to learn how to take care of me, too, in the midst of all the "stuff."

4. LEAPIN' LIZARDS II

Our family eventually settled into a routine, after overcoming the initial challenges that naturally arose from throwing two completely different families together! One issue we needed to come to terms with was what kind of talk was acceptable--and what was not.

Now, I don't think for a minute that "li'l orphant" Annie was cursing when she cried out, "Leapin' Lizards!" At our house, we have had some laughs--and tears--deciding what is crossing the line with our speech, though!

Take, for example, words like "darn" or "shoot." What do those words actually mean? I started growing uneasy when I realized that often I used the comparatively tame words to replace other less desirable words that had been part of my vocabulary at one time. Hearing a three year old spout them seems to bring home the truth, especially when accompanied by the same tone of voice and facial expression found on a sailor!

Even worse, I noticed my children using words I felt were abbreviations for taking the Lord's Name in vain. I hated hearing, "Geez," which was probably the one that made my skin crawl the most. It was just too close to saying our precious Lord's Name, Jesus, and it was forbidden in our house.

It wasn't just those words, though; I was

growing tired of so much bathroom talk! The boys were the greatest offenders here. Even after my warnings, they continued to gleefully roll words off their tongues describing bodily functions! I knew something had to give regarding our conversations at home.

    We decided to try a coin jar. Anyone who used a forbidden word had to put in a nickel. This came in handy for other types of offenses, too, such as speaking unkindly to a family member, making fun of another person, calling names, back talking parents, or even cussing--all related to issues of the mouth and priced accordingly. As a person paid his fine, he also had to place a mark beside his name on the provided card. At the end of a designated time period, the person with the least marks received the contents of the jar.

    Talk about motivation! It was blissfully quieter at our house! Polly, already normally the silent type, barely spoke for over a month! At the end, she and Tracy tied, so they split the money between them. It was a sizeable amount--about $26 or so. It just didn't seem fair, though, since Tracy was usually gone to work or out in the garage, and Polly was so quiet normally. Okay, you guessed it; only Sara and I complained about it being unfair, which I still say had nothing to do with the fact that we had the most points! We *are* the most vocal in our family, and if we had been quieter, they all would have missed the *blessings* that came out of our mouths, too!

The jar was only one of many ideas we eventually adopted to try to lovingly discipline our crew. Obviously, having that many people in the house created many additional chores, and I was still teaching full-time. Not only did I need help, but Tracy and I firmly believe that work is very good for children, and they gain tremendous responsibility and concern for others as they learn to carry part of the work load and apply some elbow grease.

They don't naturally warm up to the idea of work, though! Once again, there must be motivation! We couldn't afford hefty allowances, so after reading several sources and combining the ideas I thought would work, we employed a list based on earned points. We experimented until we found a workable plan for our family, and we still occasionally use it with the school-aged children. The points are used at the end of the week to determine what kinds of privileges the children enjoy!

There are four levels of privileges: level four gives the most freedom, with two special activities with friends (such as a sleep-over, skating, etc.), a $5 allowance, unlimited play outside or swimming in season, free television/video privileges (within guidelines of what is appropriate), and a later bedtime. The levels gradually lessen until, at level one, the child has an early bedtime, there is no allowance, special privileges are non-existent, and so on.

Do I think the kids will begin to think their

worth depends on what they do? No! They are still loved no matter what level they're on, and we have family times that everyone enjoys, regardless of his level for that week. But the children do know that there are consequences for their actions, and they are the only ones who can determine the outcome of their privileges. In this decade of victims, I think it's refreshing to try to instill within our children the concept that they have some control over what happens to them! (They could give lessons to the White House on taking consequences!)

People often ask what we do with our adult children who live at home. It didn't take long to discover that they would like to enjoy the privileges of adulthood, such as staying up late, going where they please, choosing how to spend their time, and so on, without the responsibilities of adulthood, like doing some laundry, helping with the meals and dishes, scrubbing the bathroom--you get the picture! After asking innumerable times for help--to no avail--I decided to start charging rent to the two older girls who had graduated from high school. We decided $300 a month was a fair price for room and board, laundry service, and the other comforts we provided.

The key was, the girls could work off the rent, and I hoped they would, since I needed their help more than their money! The going rate for cleaning help in our area was $10 an hour. This amounted to the girls helping an average of one hour a day in place of their rent. It didn't matter to me when they chose to work during the week, but on Saturday night, whatever hours remained unworked became payable immediately.

    They hated this plan! They cried, complained, and threatened to move out! They compared their hard lives with those of their privileged friends! They tested the rules to see if we could possibly mean it! (We did!) I can still vividly remember one weekend when Sara had chosen to spend every evening and all day Saturday with her boyfriend, Danny. Late Saturday night, she informed me that they were going to a Christian concert Sunday evening in Wichita. I responded that it sounded like lots of fun, and would she please pay me her $70 for the week since she hadn't taken time to work.

    Her eyes became rounded saucers and her mouth dropped open! She informed me that she didn't have any money, and she'd do the work later the next week. I knew it wouldn't go over well, but I had to let Sara know that we didn't extend credit. If she couldn't afford the money, she would have to schedule her free time to include doing her work at home. I told her she couldn't go to the concert unless her hours were in for the previous week. She was hopping mad! Tracy backed me up, and we were so pleased with Danny when he also showed his support! She stayed up *really* late Saturday night, and we agreed to give her credit for whatever hours Danny could contribute, too. The next afternoon before she left for the concert, she finished her hours.

Sara was still upset with us when she left for the evening, but we believe it was a valuable lesson. All of us need balance in our lives. We can't play all the time! We have responsibilities, and we must learn to live within our means. I'm still waiting for the day when she thanks me, but I know it will come--probably when she has older teenagers of her own! Meanwhile, I'm trying to learn the flip side of the lesson; we also aren't balanced if we don't take some time off to relax and "play" a bit. I find it so difficult to schedule fun, knowing the work will all be waiting for me when I'm done!

We occasionally need a break from our "lists" and point systems. Any idea can eventually lose its novelty, and this was also true of the coin jar. We tried various other methods to curb vocal naughties, but none stands out in my memory as much as the mouth washings.

Now, my mother *never* washed our mouths out with soap! I patterned much of my parenting after her, but I was growing desperate, and several friends had suggested I try washing mouths. So, with thorough, serious warning, I informed the children that if they couldn't keep their words under control, I would have to make it so unpleasant for them that they'd *want* to talk nicely!

It didn't take long for that warning to be tested, and my resolve with it. I know children can tell when you really don't want to go through with consequences, but I felt I had to be firm. Nathan and

Ben were the first offenders, talking about bodily functions repeatedly, and I was as queasy as they were when I insisted that they open their mouths to receive the orange liquid soap I had waiting for them. I made them hold it in their mouths for a few seconds, then allowed them to wash it out. It did curb their language for awhile, but I cried harder than they did. I only used this method a handful of times, but I have to grudgingly admit that it worked wonders--and quickly!

After deciding to follow Jesus at eighteen years of age, I went for years without cursing. As the pressures of life began to weigh down a few months after the children arrived, though, I occasionally caught myself with a "bad" word on my lips. I hated it, and even after much prayer, I seemed to find little victory. If I'd had any guts at all, I'd have made myself wash my *own* mouth out with soap!

The truth is, ". . . out of the abundance of the heart, the mouth speaketh." (Matthew 12:34) Changing the outside does little for changing the inside. I found that for the first time in a long time, I was harboring ill feelings and bad attitudes about my situation in life. I was overworked, underpaid, (ha!), and over committed--and I was giving the best years of my life to a couple of kids who really didn't want what I had to offer. Polly and Jeri didn't want "new parents," and although I understood why, it still didn't lessen the pain. In my humanity, hurt feelings and the deep desire to be accepted surfaced. I resented the rejection of my love and affection, and it took years for me to work through those issues--I'm not sure I'm done yet! I have, though, learned to give the girls to Jesus and trust His will and His way and His timing. He really does make all things beautiful in His time, and He does a good job of cleaning up the inside so that what comes out is pleasant, too.

5. LEAPIN' LIZARDS III

Unlike stories I've heard of other young males, my boys have never been much on bringing things home in their pockets; not many snakes, lizards, or other live, creepy, slimy, smelly things have shown up in the laundry baskets.

Other things show up in the laundry, however, such as ink pens, lipstick, markers, (never until they've completed the dry cycle, though, and have become forever bonded by heat into the one new name-brand pair of jeans one child has used his or her hard-earned money to purchase!) and money. I finally tired of asking, threatening, and begging the children to check their pockets. Now, anything left in the laundry becomes my property, and the perpetrator owes me $5 just for pulling up with it! It's amazing how much a little financial incentive will affect the kids' behaviors!

As far as the creepy crawlers go, though, we've not had much excitement when it comes to the boys bringing in surprises--nor the girls, for that matter. We have, however, had our share of critters to fight. Take, for instance, that battle with head lice we fought right when the children moved in.

I don't know how much you know about head lice, but they are tiny bugs that lay eggs in the hair, and they itch like crazy. Not only that, but they are extremely *easy* to pass to others and extremely *hard* to get rid of! You can't just treat the infected people; no, to ensure proper disposal of the critters, you must treat every head in the house *and* treat the entire *house*. This might sound easy to you, but there were nine of us, and we lived in a tri-level home that had over 4,000 square feet! Even though the children had just moved in, since they had been all over the house, I knew the lice could be anywhere--and probably were! Just sitting on a sofa or chair, or placing a sweater next to someone else's clothing or on the carpet, could spread the infectious little critters. So, even though the "original" Spencers didn't have any evidence of lice, to be safe, I treated everyone.

    I started by shooing everybody out of one bedroom upstairs, then I disinfected that room completely. I had to strip every bed, vacuum the mattresses and carpets and furniture, treat the stuffed animals, etc.--nothing could be left to chance! Then I began treating the children. All three of our foster daughters had long, thick hair, and after treating with special shampoo, it had to be combed out with a metal comb with teeth as tight as your Aunt Hilda's bank account! I went through the routine with a couple of kids so they'd have somebody to talk to, placed them in the disinfected room, and moved to the next room. This procedure, going back and forth from the house to the children, and finally ending with treating Tracy and myself, continued from 8:00 A.M. on a Saturday till about 3:00 A.M. Sunday.

    That might not seem too bad, except that in a

week's time, you must re-treat! If you will check the picture of Tracy, you'll understand why he didn't think he needed re-treating (he's not got a lot of hair!), but to be thorough, the rest of us and the house had to be redone. To make matters worse, there were still nits visible in the hair of the foster children. Nits are the eggs the lice leave behind, with the potential for many more little critters! I continued to re-treat every Saturday for six weeks straight.

Finally, in desperation, I took the matter up with our children's pediatrician. When he discovered how long I'd been treating, he began to chuckle. I remained unamused and glowered at him through the dark circles under my eyes, but his chuckle turned into a chortle as he informed me that if I'd treated thoroughly for six weeks, nothing could be alive! Needless to say, I didn't share his ability to see the humor, but I *did* get some sleep that weekend, and we've not had another episode since!

We have had another battle on our hands, though: mice! Our three-story home, in a rural community of about 1,000 people, is on the edge of town, only a block away from wheat fields. For you city-slickers, of which I was one, this means that when harvest occurs, the little mice who have lived happily in the fields all season suddenly need new homes, and ours is so nearby, it only stands to reason that they'd try us first! Our home is about 100 years old, and *not* weather-tight, so there's easy access in the little cracks under doors, etc. Every year, right after harvest in the summer, then again in the fall when the temperature begins to drop, we have these little visitors. I guess my reputation for hospitality has reached the rodent community, because one tiny mouse came right in our front door while we watched!

I'm not terribly squeamish anymore (how can you be with this many children?!), and I'm not particularly frightened of mice (spiders are another matter!), but these rodents take you by surprise. We can be sitting in the livingroom, working on someone's homework or sharing a family video, when a couple of us notice a faint movement out of the corner of our eyes. Mice are fast, so you can't be sure you even saw anything at first, but eventually, they reveal themselves directly, which is preferred, or indirectly, which is not pleasant since it means they leave evidence that they've been helping themselves to something from your kitchen cupboards, and the result known as "droppings" is left behind.

We've tried all the remedies, short of having the Orkin man visit! We've set the old-fashioned traps with cheese, we've put out more humane sticky sheets for them to adhere to, we've left D-Con in their paths, and we've chased them with brooms! I must admit I begin to feel a little sorry for them--they're kind of cute--but then the reality of dangers from the Hanta virus carried by rodents comes back to me, and I know I must consider the health of the children, so the chase is on again. We always have a temporary victory until the next harvest, when they seem to sense the welcome mat is back out, and we start over.

Thinking of little boys and the smelly things they seem to enjoy reminds me of our first Easter with the children. Ben was seven and Justin was four. We'd enjoyed a wonderful day with my family, including hunting Easter eggs. Now, we don't get into the Easter bunny or any such thing, but we think it's a fun game to hide eggs and find them, all the time letting the children see that we adults are hiding the eggs they themselves colored the day before! We always eat a good share of the eggs after counting to be sure we've found all of them, and after the fun, the remaining eggs go into the refrigerator to await their fate as egg salad sandwiches.

Well, this particular year, I didn't count as carefully to be sure the number of eggs in the fridge matched the total colored minus what we'd eaten. With seven children to keep track of, it didn't seem as important, and I was just glad we got home with all the *children* we left with!

A couple of days after Easter, I began to notice a strange odor in Ben and Justin's room. I wondered if Justin had accidentally wet his bed and not told me, but the sheets were dry. I searched through the toy box, but didn't find any creepy crawler drawing his last breath, so I shrugged it off. Well, a couple of days more, when I went to retrieve clean underwear for Justin as he came out of the tub, I realized the smell had gone from strange to horrid. I discovered the culprit: the boys had stashed extra Easter eggs in their underwear drawer in case they wanted a snack in the night! Thankfully, they hadn't eaten any of them, or the Hanta virus would have seemed like a vacation!

I can't say that the boys are *totally* responsible for "gross" things at our house; the conversation quickly goes to bodily functions (yes, still!), and the girls have learned to hang right in there with the boys. This seems to be a trait of many big families-- at least it was with mine! As the oldest of six children, no subject was off limits when I was at home. I have to admit that being a songwriter, I'm just as challenged as the children to come up with new verses to the diarrhea song! Okay, I admit we're gross, but we have lots of fun, and it's cheap entertainment--something that's a precious commodity at our house! If somebody wants to finance a trip to Worlds of Fun Amusement Park, we'll lay aside our bathroom humor for awhile for more appropriate entertainment, but meanwhile, try to understand--and maybe even laugh with us! Now, please excuse me; the earlier talk of lice makes me need to scratch!

6. LEAPING FLAMES

    We have been privileged to take a few trips with our children. One of our most memorable experiences was the time our van caught on fire! We were en route to Paola, Kansas, to visit our dear friends, the D'Ursos, when Tracy was pulled over for speeding. I typically nagged Tracy any time he exceeded the speed limit, *or* I sat in smug silence, lips pursed in a thin line to let him know that even though I was holding my tongue, he would surely get stopped and it would serve him right. He would blow our budget, thus learning his lesson. I, though, would still have to suffer while I tried to figure out how to make ends meet, and there was no way I was going to suffer alone! Just the right wag of my head and insufferable sigh, while piercing him with my eyes over the top of my book and under my raised eyebrows every few miles was enough to let him know that I was aware of his lead foot.

    Well, the officer didn't go right to the ticket. Instead, he asked Tracy if he was burning lots of oil in the van, because he'd noticed some smoke coming from our vehicle. They opened the hood and the flames went leaping! I opened the side door of the van and began pitching children out onto the ground as quickly as I could, with instructions for them to move away! The highway patrolman helped Tracy put out the flames, but we had to have the van towed to the

D'Urso's house and finally pulled home. It was ruined. I guess the officer decided we'd had enough trouble, because he didn't issue Tracy a ticket!

I mention the D'Urso family with much fondness. I actually met Liz and Geoff in Sterling, Kansas, before I met Tracy. All four of us were students at the Jesus Academy, a non-accredited Bible school where we learned to walk with Jesus. Geoff and Tracy lived in a boarding house together, and Liz and I shared a trailor with two other girls. Those relationships we built when we were all finding our identities in Jesus Christ are priceless! We have gone through many trials together, and the love we share has stood the test of over twenty years.

The same is true of our friends Steve and Robbie Petitfils. Robbie was also a student at the Jesus Academy, and when our family spent two years in San Angelo, Texas, she and her Steve were nearby in Abilene. We met Steve during that time and have been fast friends ever since, even though we're back in Kansas and they're between Houston and Galveston now.

Not only have we continued to stay in touch through the miles as the Lord has led us to different parts of the country, but the Lord has led each of us to adopt! Liz was adopted as an infant, and now she and Geoff have adopted a precious little girl, after raising their three boys. Steve and Robbie adopted their oldest son, Jacob, and added a birth son, Luke, to the family. We find ourselves on the road to see them whenever we can go, and vice versa!

My dear friend, Connie, who told us about Loving Homes, goes way back to our days in Sterling, too. She and her husband, Bruce, have adopted all three of their children: Rob, Beth, and Vanessa. When they were pastoring in Pueblo, Colorado, we were able to visit a few times. They're in Minnesota now, so we have to settle for letters and occasional phone calls or *quick* visits when they're in Kansas to see relatives.

We've gone through thick and thin with these families, and they are very important to our adopted children, as well as to the rest of us. These are people who know us well, faults and all, and love us anyway! They have been through the rigors of adoption and survived! They are true friends who mean the world to all of us! Wish those road trips could be more frequent!

Other trips have also been important, like the one we took the first summer we shared with the children. Dear Hulse and Carol Wagner, of Wichita Falls, Texas, invited us to spend the week with them in their cabin in Colorado. What a glorious vacation-- one we've never been able to top! Hulse and Carol fed us, watched the three youngest children so the older ones and Tracy and I could attend meetings, and generally took care of us. Hulse is a child psychologist, so I'm sure it was of special interest to him to watch our family interacting and growing together in those first months. "Uncle" Hulse and

"Aunt" Carol will never know how much it meant to us to have that time together in the mountains. Thank you again, dear friends! We still love the Rocky Mountains and when possible, the children and Tracy accompany me when I meet with my record company each summer during Praise in the Rockies.

We always go to Houston as often as possible to see Grandma Spencer and Aunt Patsie, Tracy's mother and sister. When weather permits, we head for Galveston to swim in the gulf and gather sea shells. We keep the two of them running while we shop at the terrific malls, watch ice skating at the Galleria, and eat our fill of authentic Tex-Mex food! Grandma Spencer especially loves taking us to visit her church, where her brothers and sisters in Christ are truly her family.

The year Dad Spencer died, as we traveled back to Kansas from his funeral, we stopped at a little restaurant called Ponte's Diner. It's located in Fairfield, Texas, and is a favorite of the locals, with its 'fifties nostalgia and jukebox. The food is incredible, and our first visit there proved to be a priceless find: not only did we discover a place where all of us could eat something we enjoyed, but we met a waitress named D'Lynn.

D'Lynn was a young thing--late teens or early twenties--scurrying around, hurrying to turn in orders and deliver plates of food in her efficient style. She was obviously tired, but gave us good service. There was something about her that caught my attention;

I'm still not sure exactly what it was. Maybe it was the determination I saw in her young eyes. Perhaps it was the fragile soul I sensed behind her busy exterior. At any rate, I ended up leaving her a nice tip with our names and address. I was delighted when she actually wrote to us! We've continued to correspond ever since, and we've been so proud of her accomplishments as she's gone to school while holding down at least one job--sometimes two! When we travel to Texas now, the children always eagerly postpone their meal if we're nearing Fairfield; we know it doesn't matter *when* we eat--only *with whom* we eat when we're going to see D'Lynn!

Studies show that traveling can actually increase I.Q.; I'm not sure if it's true or not, but it sure makes sense to me! Not only do we stretch and learn and grow on these trips, but such wonderful memories are built! We play games on the way, like trying to find license plates from all fifty states, or going through the entire alphabet, spotting the A-B-C's on billboards and signs. Getting away from the phone and jobs and projects at home is important refreshing time, and we wish we could go more. Thank the Lord for providing friends and family to visit!

When I think of the flames in the burning van, I can't help but think of other flames that have plagued us. In particular, the childhood saying, "Liar, liar, pants on fire," comes to mind. My children have learned that lying will get them into more trouble with me than anything else they could do! Everyone errs and sins and makes mistakes; that's a given. But to lie about it--ugh! Nothing bothers me more! I think there's a spiritual reason for that. Satan is referred to as the "father of lies" in Scripture--not the father of lust or stealing or greed, or any other vice. Jesus, on the other hand, is referred to as "the Way, the Truth, and the Life." He is truth embodied! There is something so deep about being honest, and the same is true of lying. It matters that we admit when we're wrong, even if it means facing consequences. We want to be children of the day, children of the Lord, not hiding in darkness with deceit. Lord, help me be an example to my children, completely and utterly honest, even when it hurts!

One more thing that flames remind me of: martyrdom! Saints of old were burned at the stake for their faith. I used to tell Liz D'Urso that if I had to experience death before the Lord Jesus returned for His children, I wanted to go as a martyr. We had many conversations about this, and she always wanted to opt for the "dying in her sleep of old age" path, if given any vote on the matter. All those years ago, I thought myself terribly noble, but since then I've learned that my willingness to die for Christ is largely part of my personality and makeup. I tend to perceive myself as a martyr, the one who is willing to go the extra mile, sacrificing myself for others, even dying to my own needs and wants--not a noble quality when the motivation is to draw attention to self! I can easily overemphasize the sacrifices I make for others, and I like to be sure Tracy and the children notice and give me credit for it! Yucky!

The Lord Jesus *died* for all of us, and even when those He died for reviled Him, He didn't retaliate or become bitter. No, He asked the Heavenly Father to forgive them! What conviction for me! I need to continue to give to others without any expectations in return--nor any desire to be recognized. My sacrifices don't even begin to compare with His, yet I take offense so easily when mine are rejected. When my two oldest adopted children don't want me, I want to whine and have somebody feel sorry for me. I want to shout, "Don't you know what I've done for you? Don't you see how I've given up my time and energy and health? Can't you see that I'm not the mother I used to be to my birth children? Why do you reject me? All I've ever wanted is to love you and have that love returned. I've wanted only good for you, but you haven't been willing to receive what I have to give you. We can't get back those years that are gone! Will there ever come a day when you'll see how much I care and let me in your hearts?"

Lord, forgive me! Help me keep loving and giving even when I see no results. Give me patience as You do Your work in Your time--as the girls let *You* in. Give me the grace I need to release them, even if it means they never become part of the picture I have painted in my mind of what our family could be. Keep the flames of Your refining fire burning within me, changing me and making me more like Jesus.

7. THE BABE LEAPED IN HER WOMB

This phrase, ". . . the babe leaped in her womb," is found in a passage of Scripture in Luke 1 where Elizabeth received a visit from Mary, who had just learned she was with child. Elizabeth was expecting John the Baptist, and when Mary approached, John leaped inside Elizabeth. He leaped for joy, and Elizabeth was filled with the Holy Spirit, exclaiming what she knew to be true--that Mary was expecting their Lord and Savior!

Pregnancy is such a special time in a woman's life! Knowing that a life is growing within you is beyond awesome--such a miracle! Although I have a house full of children, it has not always been so. In fact, there was a time when Tracy and I thought we might never have children at all.

Soon after we married, we decided to start our family. Many of our friends were having babies, and we knew children were truly a blessing from the Lord. Not too long after our decision, I was pretty sure I was pregnant. The pregnancy test was negative, though; in those days, the urine test was the most common, and it wasn't always accurate. When symptoms still seemed to indicate a pregnancy, I decided to have an examination. The doctor who examined me assured me that even though the test had been negative, he could tell I was expecting. He said that the size and condition of my uterus confirmed the pregnancy, and Tracy and I were ecstatic! Our joy was short-lived, though, when I began cramping and bleeding. Sure enough, our fears were founded; I had miscarried our baby.

Not too many months later, I conceived again, only to lose this baby, as well. I was overcome with depression. Not only were all my friends getting pregnant--even one who wasn't trying to be--but my young faith was being shaken. I knew God was big enough and well able to sustain my pregnancies, and children are a gift from Him. Did that mean that since I wasn't able to carry my babies, He was upset with me? Did it mean His blessing wasn't on my life? Had I sinned in some way I couldn't discover? Was He not as involved with our daily lives as I'd been taught?

All of these questions plagued me, and when I conceived again, I was a nervous mother-to-be, waiting for the bottom to drop out of my world again. Even with some bleeding, though, I was able to carry this child to term, and we were blessed with our precious Sara Jenae on January 7th, 1979. What a joy she was to me, somehow letting me know that God didn't have anything personal against me! Of course, this was immature faith, for His love for us and acceptance of us is based on His Word, not on outward blessings or circumstances!

When we began to think it was time to add a little brother or sister for Sara, I miscarried three more times. My heart was grieved each time, but back then, I couldn't get my doctor to listen to me. He seemed to think that since I'd already carried one baby to term, infertility wasn't an issue to be concerned with. I was hurt by what seemed to be his calloused insensitivity, but didn't know how to express my need to validate my losses, nor how to cope with my fears when, once again, I experienced bleeding and cramping during my seventh pregnancy.

Thankfully I was able to carry our good-natured Nathan Jon, born January 27th, 1982, to term, and our joy knew no limits! Both children were well-behaved and happy, and I was sure I must deserve the mother of the year award! Ha! Little did I know that their good behavior had as much to do with their temperaments as with any parenting skills I possessed!

I've already mentioned having two teenaged girls live with us, and it was when Nathan was a toddler that I received a phone call from thirteen year old Angie. We'd met her once before when a local pastor had asked us if she and her mother and two younger siblings could stay at our house to hide from her abusive stepfather. We agreed and met them, but hadn't heard anymore from them since that weekend--until Angie's call.

Angie was concerned because her twelve year old sister, LeAnn, whom we hadn't yet met, was planning to run away from home. I quickly made arrangements for the two girls to come over to talk, since I knew firsthand what happened to runaways, having had a sister who had run away from home as a teenager. Cathy, four years younger than I, learned the hard way that some very bad people are waiting like vultures to see run-away girls catching the bus or train. These people feign concern and make the girls who are estranged from their families feel that they have finally found a true friend--one who understands them and wants to help. These tricksters take the girls under wing, only to use them in the worst way and show them a side of life that most of us think only exists in "D" movies. If I could save LeAnn from making the mistakes Cathy had made, I certainly wanted to do so.

    To make a long story short, I invited Angie and LeAnn to spend a few days with us while things cooled off at home. When I called their mother to be sure it was okay, she asked if we would let the girls live with us, but we were sure that after having a break from each other and the situation, all parties involved would be ready to make amends and live together again. I suggested a two-week trial period, during which they could all calm down and decide what was best.

    At the end of the two weeks, their mother still wanted us to keep the girls, so she gave us legal guardianship of them. Angie and LeAnn lived with us for three years; at the end of that time, their step-father was in prison, making it more desirable for them to go home. We made arrangements for their reunion with their mother, a decision that was born out of our desire to see them whole. Most children are more stable and secure and happy in their family of origin, even when it isn't the environment many of us would consider normal or healthy. Those family ties are strong. We can see now that the girls' mother gave them up out of her love for them, not wanting them to be hurt, but not able to leave her abusive husband, either. Once the danger to them was eliminated, it was a good thing for them to bond again with their birth mother.

During the girls' stay with us, I conceived again! This was the most difficult pregnancy yet, with lots of bleeding. My doctor was out-of-town during one bad episode, and the doctor on call was sure I had miscarried again. He wanted me to go in for a D & C, but somehow I didn't have peace about it and wanted to wait for my own doctor to return. How thankful we have been for that decision, because my doctor ordered a sonogram and I was still pregnant! Our baby was kicking away! I had to rest in bed and take things easy for awhile, and the pregnancy was touch and go for the first few months, but on January 24, 1995, Benjamin Wayne joined our family, bringing even more laughter to our home with his adorable sense of humor.

While I was still pregnant with Ben, an unusual thing happened. We had a time of fellowship in our home, and our friend, Pastor John Hollar, began to pray for our family. The tone shifted, though, and he started to voice what I believe was actually a New Testament-type prophecy. He said that Tracy would be the father of many more children than he could see then! We weren't sure what to make of it, but we knew in our hearts that the Lord had really spoken to us, so we just treasured the words, writing them in our journals, and waiting for the Lord to move. We didn't know it would be seven years before those words brought forth fruit, and it wasn't until after we got our precious adopted children that we remembered the prophecy! When we got the children, we thought that was the end of the story, that God had given us those many children He had foretold and we were done.

Not quite! Since I'd had so much trouble carrying children, and we were pretty sure the adoption was going to go through, we decided in June of 1993 that Tracy should have a vasectomy. After all, seven children was quite a houseful! Knowing that my chances of carrying another child full-term were slim, we decided to do something permanent. Makes sense, doesn't it? Well, not to the Lord! His ways are not our ways, and His thoughts are not our thoughts!

I didn't know it at the time, but a dear sister in Christ, Coleen, was praying fervently that the surgery wouldn't work--and it didn't! Tracy and I could hardly believe it, and the doctor offered to repeat the surgery free of charge, but we felt that we needed to give the Lord an opportunity to work in this area of our lives. It seemed that if we were supposed to be done with babies, the surgery would have worked the first time!

I conceived immediately, and we were overjoyed! I was almost past the twelve week "danger zone" and hadn't experienced any trouble with the pregnancy. That joy was crushed, though, when at eleven weeks, I began bleeding heavily. Dr. George Cullan was on call, and had to inform me that I was probably going to miscarry. He was compassionate, gentle, supportive, and Tracy and I felt we'd finally found a doctor we could really trust. There were many ups and downs, not knowing whether or not I would be able to carry this baby. We thought I had lost the child, but our sonogram showed it was still living. Next thing we knew, I was bleeding again, and a repeated sonogram revealed life was gone. I finally agreed to a D & C.

It was a nightmare! The other pregnancies had terminated early enough that I was able to pass all "tissue" without the need for the procedure, but this time, days were turning into weeks, and I was too exhausted and sick to wait it all out. The outpatient surgery was performed, and I was taken to be watched for a few hours to none other than--you guessed it--the maternity ward. My room was right next door to the nursery, so all day, I could hear the babies crying and the proud parents and grandparents pointing out which child belonged to them. I cried inconsolably.

This loss was even greater than the previous

ones, because our other children were old enough this time to share our joy and excitement. We'd shown the children books about what the baby looked like each week and how big it was; it was a family event. I wept not only for myself, but for the disappointment of each one of us.

Thankfully, Dr. Cullan didn't leave me alone in my sorrow. He asked me a myriad of questions and listened to my story. He took notes on every detail of the previous miscarriages and began intensive testing to try to find out why I had lost those babies. Eventually, he discovered I was low on progesterone, a hormone necessary to sustain the pregnancy during the first twelve weeks until the placenta takes over. He tried a drug therapy, which did a number on my hormones and made me really hard to live with, but I miscarried four more times, the last time in February of 1995.

This brought the total to ten lost babies. I'd had it. I told Tracy I couldn't try anymore. Thank God for my husband, who knows me better than anyone else does--and even better than I know myself sometimes. He asked me tenderly, "Just one more time, Bec?" I grudgingly agreed, but with the understanding that if we lost another baby, I was done, and it would be *his* turn!

Honestly, I also let the Lord know I didn't plan on trying anymore if this time didn't work. I knew that He worked everything out for my good because I loved Him. (Romans 8:28) Even the losses we'd experienced were used for good, creating in Tracy and I the awareness of how special each child is. We probably wouldn't have had the hearts for our adopted children if we hadn't suffered the losses. I was just tired, though, physically, emotionally, and spiritually. I hurt so badly that I didn't think anymore good could come of another loss.

I remember telling the Lord that if this trial was some kind of Job lesson or testing thing, then I must be pretty slow, because I obviously wasn't learning the lesson or passing the test. If I had been "getting" it, I surely would have matured past the point of needing to repeat that particular lesson so many times! I felt as though there was this huge "Hello?" bellowing down from heaven! Like, "Is anybody home down there? Are you clicking?"

It's important to note here that I went to an all-night prayer meeting in June of 1995 to ask for prayer for my father's battle with leukemia. During prayer, one woman put her hand on my shoulder and prayed silently. A warmth--even a gentle burning--radiated from her hands all through my body, and at the time, I thought it was significant for Daddy, that perhaps he would be healed. My experiences in the coming weeks led me to believe otherwise.

Dr. Cullan wanted me to come in for a test at the first suspicion of pregnancy, even if I didn't think I was really pregnant. Sure enough, July of 1995, I was a couple of days late on my cycle, but felt crampy like I would probably start anytime. I felt foolish going in for a pregnancy test, and told Cheryl, Dr. Cullan's nurse, that it was a waste of time. I had learned that the urine tests I had taken years before sometimes showed negative due to the hormonal deficiency I had, so a blood test was ordered. A few hours after returning home from the blood test, Cheryl called.

Her first words were, "Light the candles!" I was in shock and couldn't quite catch her meaning. She assured me, though, that indeed my pregnancy test was positive! Dr. Cullan had me go back into town to pick up a prescription for progesterone that same afternoon, and I began therapy immediately.

This pregnancy was completely problem-free! Even the delivery was by the book! In my other deliveries, I'd never had the urge to push--the nurses would have to tell me when to do my part. I'd warned Dr. Cullan about this, but during this delivery, he almost missed the event! With my husband, Tracy, our oldest daughter, Sara, and my mother present, I delivered our beloved Anna Marie on March 25th, 1996. Was it the progesterone or the prayers or even some chiropractic work I'd had done? I don't know-- probably a combination of all three--but I thank the Lord Jesus for our little one, spoiled though she may become!

Anna has been good for all of us. When I first held her in my arms, my heart was healed of the pain of losing the other babies. She brought us all together, being *everybody's* baby. We thought the

Lord was wise to let us model for our children the important steps of pre-natal care, how to care for an infant, and how to teach a toddler to obey.

Still, having Anna seemed almost too good to be true. For the first full year, I braced myself for pain, feeling that after all the heartache we'd experienced with the other pregnancies, perhaps something would yet go wrong. People had warned me that at the "old age" of 39, my risk of having a baby with a birth defect was much greater. My heart overflowed with relief at the hospital when we learned that she was completely healthy, but I carefully communicated my willingness to go through whatever trial the Lord might send my way, even if it meant a less than healthy child as she grew. I asked Him to forgive me for my lack of faith during fearful moments, yet I felt Him speaking to my heart that faith is trusting in Him even when life *doesn't* go the way we expect or want it to. After that first year, I let myself begin to relax and just enjoy Anna.

One thing I've never been able to understand is the reaction of many people when they learn we have eight children. It was one thing for us to have the three and adopt a family of four, bringing the total to seven. After all, they reason, we wouldn't have wanted to split up the family of children we adopted. But they act like it's insane to have wanted another baby! In fact, people would give us dirty looks when I was expecting; they'd count the children piling out of our van, then I'd show up, waddling along heavy with child! Strangers would even walk up to me and ask if I realized what was causing that!

Others ask in doubt, "Are they *all yours?*" I hate feeling like I must explain that actually four are adopted and four are birth children, as though that makes it okay! We have several dear friends with large families. The Wisners have eight children, too, and they're *all* birth children! The Websters just had their seventh child! The Ablas have also had seven children! *It's okay to have a big family!*

Do I want more? No! At one point, I'd asked the Lord to give me one baby for each one I'd lost. Tracy and I agreed after Anna came that we'd count Angie and LeAnn for a total of ten--one for each of the ten children I miscarried--and we'd consider our quiver full!

Many people, upon learning we have eight children, shudder and quickly say they have only one and can hardly handle that. It's certainly okay for people to choose small families or no families at all. But how sad that in our society, children are considered a hardship and inconvenience--even a disposable item!

Lord, forgive us all.

8. TEN LORDS A-LEAPING

I always have to double-check the words to remember which verse this is in the famous "Twelve Days of Christmas" song. Our first Christmas together with the children needs no reminder, though! We'd only had them for two months, and they had been in the paper a lot, so the community knew about them and wanted to reach out. People were extremely generous with the children, and we couldn't thank them enough for the way they made the kids' first Christmas without their parents special.

Gifts began to show up, and the area under our tree was quickly full. Betty Parker contacted Dillons Stores, who gave us several bushels of food, soap, and other goodies. She had also been bringing over her wonderful desserts since the kids' arrival, and that continued during the holidays. A few people brought fruit baskets, and folks were just generous overall.

The only thing that wasn't considered by everyone was that our family had three other children! Some people were sensitive to this, but not all even realized it. Naturally, they were concerned for the four children facing their first Christmas without their parents, and that was the proper focus. But my birth children were beginning to struggle to keep the right attitudes.

One dear woman had invited us out to see her horses, and she produced presents for the four children to open. They were excited, and went ahead and opened them right there so the kind woman and her husband could enjoy watching; none of us really realized that the three birth children were bothered. Shortly, Ben, who was only six at the time, asked where his present was! The woman realized what had happened, and quickly went to hunt for additional gifts, but she only found something for Ben and Nathan. She apologized to Sara and felt truly awful about it, but it couldn't be helped at that point. We reassured her that it was fine, and Sara tried hard to be mature, but at twelve years old, she was being stretched to the limit!

When we got into the van, Sara was stiff and quiet until Polly mentioned she hoped she got a headphone set for Christmas. That was the straw that broke the camel's back! Sara unleashed her frustration, letting Polly know that of course she'd get it--she obviously got everything else she wanted! Sara ranted and raved for a couple of minutes before locking eyes with me, seeing in my expression that I expected her to put a lid on it immediately!

When we returned home, she huffed into the house, and I followed her quickly, gently guiding her into my bedroom and closing the door. I held her, even though at first she was wooden and defiant. Eventually she relaxed a little, and I began to share. We had to remember that even though the children were receiving lots of attention at that point, including taking up lots of my time that used to be just for the birth kids, still the new kids had lost much that could never be replaced. They'd never have their mother again. They'd never known a stable home life. They'd actually lost their father, too, since he was incarcerated and they weren't allowed visits. Sara's tender heart was unveiled again, and she wept, knowing that her new siblings would have traded all the presents in a moment's time if they could have had their family back. Such hard lessons, but valuable, as all of us gained a greater understanding of what's important in life!

Most of our other Christmases have been far more normal. One family has faithfully given us $300 each year at Christmas and occasionally someone else also shares with us, enabling us to buy a special gift for each child. There was *nothing* normal about the Christmas of 1998, though!

My mother and I had opened a craft mall in December of 1997 to give her income doing something less stressful than selling advertising, which she'd been doing for some time. My father was already ill with leukemia and hadn't worked for over two years, and I wanted to help provide for their needs. Still, it had taken longer for the craft mall to get going than we'd planned, and I'd had to pour all my extra resources into it, besides borrowing all the money I could to keep it running. We literally had *no* money to go Christmas shopping that following year!

December 1st, Tracy and I called all the children into the livingroom and read the Christmas story out of Luke. We then shared with the kids that this year, there was no money to purchase gifts. We told them that if the Lord decided to bless them with presents, we'd trust Him to provide them, but if not, we were asking that they have a mature attitude about it, knowing Christmas was about our Savior's birth. The kids were great, cheerfully agreeing to accept whatever came our way--lean or plenty!

A few days later, I received a strange phone call. A gentleman informed me that he wasn't a "weirdo," but he wasn't going to tell me his name, either! He said his wife and her friend had heard me speak at a ladies' meeting, and then he explained that each year, they chose a family to "do" for Christmas. He wanted to know if we'd consider accepting being their family that year. Well, I responded that we'd been praying that if the Lord intended presents for our kids, He'd provide them, and each day, I'd been making sure the Lord knew how many days were left before Christmas! With that in mind, I told him we probably would accept!

The kind, anonymous friend asked me to make a list of our children's names and ages, along with what they might want for Christmas. He went on to say that I could go up to $100 or $200--*each*! I told him I never spent that much on each one, even in good years, but he insisted that I should just write down what they really wanted. We made arrangements for him to pick up the list, and selected a time for delivery of the packages.

The Tuesday before Christmas, the gentleman and his wife and her friend showed up at our house with none other than Santa Claus, gifts in tow! Anna, who was two-and-a-half, was allowed to open a couple of presents right then, and the rest waited for Christmas morning. These precious people had not only bought each child exactly what he or she wanted for Christmas, but they also gave them gift certificates to equal spending at least $200 on each child. They included $150 gift certificates for Tracy and I, too, and lovely cologne sets. They also handed us an envelope with twenty $100 bills! Never had we had so much at one time! The children were truly thrilled, and we had the most relaxed shopping trip of our entire lives--each person had his own money to spend, and I didn't have to mentally add each selection, trying to decide whether or not we could afford it. One evening we took the family out to eat and let each person order whatever he wanted from the menu--no limits on how high he could go! It was so much fun!

Our older birth children were never allowed to do the "Santa" thing when they were small--we didn't even discuss him much, except to say that he didn't really exist. We wanted to be thorough in their spiritual training, sure that they understood what Christmas was really about. Our little Anna, though, not only believes that Santa Claus exists, but also that he's a personal friend who actually delivered presents to her house! Am I worried about her having a warped view of Christmas? No! As she grows, we'll continue to share with her about the year that we had nothing, yet celebrated our most blessed Christmas ever. I have no doubt that we'll be able to teach her that it was our Lord's doing, with the unseen work of a few of His own special helpers! We still don't know their names, and probably never will, but if these "elves" read this, thank you again!

Since we *usually* don't have much in the way of material gifts, we try to make up for it with activities each of the twenty-four days before Christmas. I have a felt tree with twenty-four pockets, which the children open each morning in December to reveal the activity for that day. We read the Christmas story from the account of Luke in the Bible to the glow of candles and Christmas tree lights. We play Christmas charades. All year, I find t-shirts and sweatshirts in good condition at garage sales, and we spend one night painting designs on them. We listen to Christmas music while making peanut brittle. We deliver goodies to friends and neighbors. A favorite activity is the pizza/video/slumber party we share the weekend before Christmas! All in all, we enjoy being together and sharing the goodness of God in sending our four new children to us and sending His Son for all who would receive Him.

Peace on earth. And ten Spencers leaping!

9. GROWING IN LEAPS AND BOUNDS

People take one look at our growing crew and ask, "How do you do it?" They're referring to keeping eight children fed and cared for--especially interesting to them when Nathan stands up to his full 6'5" frame!

It's true that he's always hungry, and his brother Ben is quickly following in his footsteps! Even the girls are often hard to keep full, except when Jeri used to come home from her job in the kitchen at the nursing home in Buhler--she had no appetite after work!

One thing we've done for several years is plant and harvest a garden. There's nothing like our own canned green beans! Those from the grocery store are tasteless compared to home-grown! We also grow and can tomatoes, and love to try various hot peppers to experiment with the salsa we all enjoy making and consuming. Mexican food is our favorite; everybody likes it. Still, you have to wonder if we've overdone it when our Anna, at two years old, used to ask me to draw her a star, a heart, and a burrito!

Jeri and Justin are our two natural gardeners, loving the entire process of growing the vegetables. They were terribly disappointed, as I was, that we didn't get to put in a garden last year. Daddy died right when we should have been planting, and my grief consumed my energy during the weeks when we still could have eked out a humble produce section. We missed those veggies all winter, since they not only taste great, but help with our grocery budget, too.

Groceries just keep going up in price! Tracy works lots of overtime, but his wages don't seem to keep pace with the inflation of groceries. I don't buy lots of pre-packaged food, preferring to make things from scratch, which is far more nutritional, in addition to being more cost-effective. We eat lots of casseroles--pasta, rice, and beans are less expensive than meat.

My Uncle Larry, Daddy's brother, is a farmer. He farmed with my Grandpa Yates for years and has actually lived on and run the farm for a long time. Now and then he and Aunt Rosemary give us some meat, and Nathan is overjoyed! He gets real meat without a carbohydrate attached to it!

We shop at Good Will, the Salvation Army Thrift Store, and garage sales. It's really fun finding bargains, and on the rare Saturdays when Tracy doesn't work, we enjoy "junking" as our favorite date! Unfortunately, as the children get older, it's harder to find items they'll "appreciate" and wear!

Occasionally we work together to earn money for special needs. One year the children and I raked leaves so Nathan could get his basketball shoes. It was hard work, and we were all exhausted, but it's a good memory now!

I continued to teach full-time for three years after the children came to live with us, and it was really too much! I used to be a high-energy person, but my supply was quickly drained after getting everyone fed, helping with homework, and getting everyone settled in bed, only then to begin grading papers for the next day! Although the children helped with a fair share of the housework, much of it still loomed ahead each evening, and I was exhausted! For an entire year, our dear friend Linda Witt cleaned house for me once a week, or I'd never have made it!

Since Tracy was already working overtime and spending every spare minute on our ever-needy vehicles, he couldn't help much inside. We decided I should try teaching half-days, which not only gave me more time to get my housework and grading done, but it was the year Justin was in kindergarten, so we had our afternoons together, too. Still, it was too much. Tracy and I began to realize the Lord would have me quit teaching in order to be more effective at home--in other words, not such a *grouch*! I loved to teach and thoroughly enjoyed my students, so it was no small decision to turn in my resignation, but I wanted the best for my family, and knew they weren't getting my best while I served my students.

We were receiving an adoption subsidy, but with my quitting, it put us at the same income we'd had when there were only five of us. It was a huge step of faith--okay, a leap! The children no longer received free tuition to the Christian school; therefore, our expenses went up several hundred dollars a month, besides the drop in income. We knew "the Lord provides where He guides," though, so we felt good about my resigning. The years since then have been interesting!

For one thing, Tracy changed jobs and had more overtime available, which helped a lot financially. He had to begin working on the night shift, though, which meant he wasn't available to help with the family's training and upbringing. He left for work about 2:00 P.M., and got home around 3:00 A.M., missing the children altogether on school days. We prayed for three years before he was finally put on days.

Things always work out. The family I mentioned earlier that always gives us $300 at Christmas also gives us $300 when school starts each year. Someone gave us a brand new washing machine anonymously when our old one finally couldn't be fixed anymore. (If you're reading this book, thank you! It still works beautifully, and it's *so quiet*!)

Our older children who were working all helped pay their tuition so they could stay at Central Christian, and they bought their own clothes. We were so proud of their willingness to contribute to their education. Polly also occasionally took the family out to eat for a special treat.

We had driven old, run-down vehicles for almost seven years after the kids came, and Tracy was beginning to resemble them--run down himself! When both the van and the car were giving us trouble, a mechanic friend suggested that it wasn't worth putting any more money into either vehicle because of the high mileage on them--over 180,000 miles each. We really needed to get something more reliable, something newer and with fewer miles. I was desperately needing Tracy to be more available to me and the children, and I knew having a newer vehicle would free up his time spent in the garage; but our budget just couldn't take a vehicle payment.

  LeAnn, who used to live with us, said I needed to lay down my pride and ask for help. (Ouch!) I didn't think it was pride; I thought I was just being a good American, working for what we had instead of expecting or wanting someone else to help us out. She insisted that since we knew I needed to be available to take care of my family instead of working outside the home, and we believed the kids belonged in the Christian school, and we needed a newer vehicle, then we needed to communicate our needs to our brothers and sisters in Christ.

  I did so, asking several area churches if they could help us with obtaining a newer vehicle. We had a couple of responses, and we also had our income tax refund and the money from Nathan's totaling our car, so we began to look for something to get us around.

  I had developed fibromyalgia, which affects the muscles around the joints and several other painful spots. Besides the pain, fatigue usually accompanies this disease. Tracy really wanted to find a used Suburban so I could maneuver getting in and out of it easier than a full-sized van, and so I could handle driving it easier, too, since the van was really hard for me to tackle. I felt like I was fighting it every time I drove! We looked at several Suburbans, and I was convinced they were just too expensive. Tracy kept holding out for one in spite of my skepticism. One evening he asked me to go to Wichita with him, because he'd found a 1994 Suburban for only $14,900. I was sure it was an error; all the '94's we'd seen up to that point had been over $20,000. He insisted that we go, though, so I grudgingly went along for the ride. Certain it was a waste of time, I took along a good book to read so the trip wouldn't be a total loss!

Sure enough, the Suburban we saw was really only $14,900. It had hail damage which was hardly visible, and that's why the low price had been assigned to it. Both of us believed it was the vehicle for us; we signed the papers, made our down payment, and drove it home.

That left us with a decision about what to do for the children's schooling. I considered homeschooling them, but after having tutored Jeri for one summer school class, I just didn't think that was our best solution. I really didn't have the energy for it, and we knew our children needed as much stability and routine as possible. Public school wasn't an option for us, so when it was time for the children to begin football and cheerleading practice, we went ahead and sent them to Central Christian.

One thing that tested me was when Mr. Abla,

the superintendent of our school, called to offer me a teaching position. I came very close to accepting his offer! In my heart I knew it wasn't how the Lord wanted to provide. Anna was only two, my plate was already so full, and the fibromyalgia didn't allow me to cope well with a daily job. I still needed time to do the books for the craft mall and work occasionally to give my mother a day off. I truly believed the Lord wanted me to continue singing concerts and speaking to ladies' groups, too, so teaching didn't fit with the big picture. Tracy didn't want me to commit to it, either. After we'd prayed about it, he left the final decision up to me.

    I finally asked if half-days might be a possibility. I thought if I could teach afternoons, when Anna was asleep anyway, then maybe we could make it work. Mr. Abla was excited when he pulled out the schedule to show me he'd given me the hours I requested--but he'd put me on mornings instead of afternoons! We both felt awful! At any rate, I declined the position, and he and I both knew it was the right thing to do. As a family we continued to trust and pray.

    During this time, someone very dear to me rebuked me for not taking the teaching position. She thought it was obvious that the Lord was the One Who had prompted Mr. Abla to call me, and for me to decline was to reject God's answer for our finances. Oh, how I wanted to explain my heart to her! Unfortunately, my feelings were already hurt and I was struggling just to hold on to life, so my answer wasn't the gentle reply she deserved. The truth is, not every open door is the Lord's doing! Sometimes, our enemy also puts an open door in front of us. We must know how to follow the Lord's leading in our lives, not just take whatever circumstances come our way. In actuality, the teaching position was a temptation for me to meet our needs myself instead of doing what the Lord wanted me to do and trusting Him to provide.

The Bible says in John 10 that Jesus is the Good Shepherd, and that His sheep hear His voice. I trust that to be true and rest in the knowledge that He knows how to get through to me. It isn't my ability to hear, but rather His ability to speak that brings the guidance I need! Taking the teaching position would have proved disastrous to our family life. I'm thankful He showed me the way, even if it took awhile to get my attention.

Days before Central Christian's registration, we still weren't sure what to do about paying, but a dear saint who had helped us with our school fees for several years asked us how much our tuition for the first semester would run. He paid that, in addition to the fees. When second semester rolled around, he paid a chunk of that, too, and each month, the rest of the tuition we've needed has been there somehow!

Someone told me that we have many millionaires in our community, and many of them are Christians. For just a few moments I dreamed of what it would be like to be able to hire some help with the house and have Tracy home at decent hours and have our Saturdays off together. I contemplated being able to go to the grocery store to buy what we needed without counting and planning and balancing the whole way to be sure we had enough food without blowing the budget. For a moment I wondered why the Lord hadn't told these well-off saints to share their bounty with some of the less fortunate around them. Then I had to stop! I had no idea how they did their giving and it was none of my business. Tracy and I agreed to take the children, knowing we were taking on all that came with that task!

Even with our struggles, we still have so much more than almost everyone else in the world! I must be thankful at all times! Do I ever wish we could just rest from the stress of financial burdens? Sure, but doesn't everybody who works hard? We wouldn't trade our lives for anybody's, no matter how tight things get!

Now and then when things are really challenging, funds will show up in the mail unexpectedly. There are things we really ought to do to the house and yard, and a couple of the kids need braces. Life is good, though, and those things aren't eternal.

Probably more challenging than the finances is the demand on our time, though those two are often connected. We don't always do a good job of balancing priorities in this area. Tracy and I know we need time alone together, but how do you get that when there are so many needs? We trust that someday, when the children are all grown, we'll have time for each other. We have a strong foundation, but I must admit that at times, it gets shaken a bit when we haven't had time to share our lives with each other.

It's also a challenge to spend time with each child. Early on after the children came, I realized that on certain days, I hadn't even really spoken to Justin. He didn't have homework, so he didn't need my help there. He went to bed earlier than the others, so the opportunity for time with him was not as great. He was overall pretty well-behaved, so he didn't demand attention in that way. My mother, who raised six children, used to say my brother Tim often got left out, only because the "squeaky wheel gets the grease." Tim was a good kid, so he didn't demand the same attention those misbehaving did. I didn't want Justin to be left out. Yet, I'd lie awake in bed at night, trying to remember whether or not I'd asked him about his day or visited with him other than to be sure he had washed behind his ears and picked out clothes for the next day.

This is when I instigated "kid of the week." The "kid of the week" was the one who got to sit in the front seat and run errands with me. He got to lick the beaters if I was baking. This child got to play a game with me at least once in the week, and I tried to take him someplace special and find an inexpensive gift for him. We wrote to each other in a journal at least once during the week, and I was careful to be extra "huggy" with that child, perhaps giving a back rub if it were one who could receive that better than a hug. This was a real life-saver when it came to spending quality time with each child; although it only came around once every seven weeks, at least nobody was completely left out.

I wish I could say I've kept up with it, but as the kids' schedules have filled, we've slowed way down with the "kid of the week." We do eventually get to each child again, though, and I know I enjoy it as much as the children do; we're building memories that will last a lifetime, especially as we re-read our journaling to each other.

We've tried different approaches to the spiritual training of our children. Although they're in Christian school, we still believe it's primarily our responsibility to train them in the ways of the Lord. We've tried having family devotions, but that never lasts long on a daily basis, because no two days are alike at our house!

For several months we had a Bible study for our children one night a week. It was unique because *they* did the sharing. We sang awhile first, and Tracy and I shared, too, but each person came with something from God's Word that had especially spoken to him that week. We loved hearing what the Lord was teaching them, and it was a special blessing that Sara's Danny also participated, showing how important his faith is to him. She's going to be in good hands!

Now I try to do this sharing with the children at breakfast each morning before school. I still hope someday Tracy can cut back on his hours and join us during that time. Even though the kids know he is a man of God's Word, there's nothing like seeing your parents reading their Bibles and sharing precious truths God has revealed to them!

So, yes, it's a challenge to keep up with the growth and needs of our family, physically, emotionally, and spiritually. We do our best and trust the Lord, Who put us together in the first place! We can plant and water the seeds, but He's the One Who brings the increase and causes all of us to grow!

10. YOU CAUSED MY HEART TO LEAP INTO MY THROAT!

Even hearing about some of the accidents our adopted children had before they came to live with us is enough to cause my heart to leap into my throat! Ashley fell off a fence, dislocating her hip and putting her in a complete body cast. Polly was once trying to break up a cat fight with a knife, and accidentally cut Ashley's bare foot, requiring ten stitches. Jeri stepped in front of a moving vehicle and was hit. Another time she was bitten badly by a dog, leaving a scar along the side of her nose. Polly was thrown from a horse and broke her arm. They had so many scary stories to tell us!

Since we've had the kids, though, we've also had our share of incidents! With this many children, sometimes it seems things will never calm down!

Ashley was rollerblading in the park with her friend Chrissy, when she fell and fractured her wrist. That was scary enough, but the boys are the ones who have really kept us hopping.

Nathan broke his pinky finger during a football game in eighth grade. He broke his arm playing basketball at the Y.M.C.A. He broke his thumb playing football at school his junior year, and dislocated a rib playing basketball that same year. He broke his glasses more than anything, though--and it happened every time he played *anything* with his cousin Danny! We estimated he broke them at least twenty times! What a relief when he got his first pair of contacts!

Benjamin broke his collar bone jumping over some cushions when he was in first grade. He broke his pinky toe when he flipped his bike at Kanopolis Lake during one of our camping trips. He flipped from the top bunk bed to the bottom one, cracking his head and having to get stitches.

Justin's accidents are the most colorful of all! He crashed through the glass beside our front door and had to get stitches in his arm because he was running down the stairs and couldn't catch himself in time to stop. He was trying to do a backflip at the swimming pool, and didn't estimate the space correctly, so he flipped onto the concrete, missing the pool, and had to ride in the ambulance to the hospital where he received ten stitches in his head. He recently tripped on the stairs at a church we were visiting, spraining his ankle. He fractured his middle finger one day while riding his bike; he was holding a string, and Ashley stepped on it, sending him crashing! My all time favorite, though, is when he was pretending to bungee jump from a building in the park--only, of course, there was no bungee cord, so he broke his arm when he hit the ground!

You realize Sara isn't in the list of accidents; when she was small, I didn't let her do anything that could have possibly resulted in injury! She did sprain her ankle repeatedly during school sports, but when she was a small child, I was careful to screen all her activities for possible "owies." I went from being completely over-protective to not wanting to be called unless there's blood, to deciding we need to determine how *much* blood there is before getting excited!

Yes, there have been some tense moments as we've weathered the injuries the children have endured, but what gives me the greatest "jolt" is the more tender side: finding out that Sara and Danny have changed their weekend plans so that her daddy and I can have some much-needed time away from home; watching Polly receive the Good Citizen Award at her high school graduation; learning that Jeri offered to pay half the tuition of a student who was going to have to drop out of Central Christian because her parents couldn't afford the tuition anymore; hearing the song Nathan wrote for a memorial service for his friend, John Allen, who with his father, was killed in a car accident last summer; having one of the girls in Ben's class tell me he's different from typical junior high boys--so pure and kind that she really respects him; receiving a note from Ashley telling me how happy she is that she got to come and live with us; finding out that Justin befriended the new boy in the class so he wouldn't feel left out; hearing Anna singing from across the house, "Yes, Jesus loves me" in her three year old warble.

God has been so good to us. Now, please excuse me. Not only do I have a lump in my throat, but I think there's also something in my eye.

11. WALKING, LEAPING, AND PRAISING GOD!

Acts 3 tells the story of a crippled man who was taken to the temple to beg each day. One particular day, Peter and John were passing by, and he asked them for money. They looked at him intently and asked for his attention as well. They let him know they didn't have any money for him, but they'd give him what they did have: they commanded him in the Name of Jesus to rise up and walk. The man rose, walked, leaped, and praised God, for he had been healed!

We, too, have had healings at our house--not always as dramatic as this one, but just as real. It's true that back in 1981, when Sara was two-and-a-half years old, she was healed instantaneously of reflux, a condition that caused urine to go back into her kidneys, resulting in continual infections. She'd been on medications for months and had battled an allergic reaction to one medication. The doctors said that they hoped she would gain some relief as she grew to be about eight or ten years old, because the growth could cause the faulty tube to stretch out enough to allow better passage of the urine. We were told she would have to remain on medication all those years, though, and surgery was still a very real possibility. We prayed and prayed and prayed--at every opportunity at home, church, revivals, and anywhere anybody was willing to take it to the Lord.

At one particular revival meeting, we were especially impressed to take Sara forward for anointing with oil and prayer. The evangelist started laughing as we prayed, and commented after prayer that we could "take it to the bank." There seemed to be faith in the room that night that whatever we asked of God, He was going to do.

I called Dr. Ted Grimes, a fellow believer, the next morning, and asked him to repeat Sara's test to show whether or not there had been a healing. He agreed, and there was *no sign of reflux!* She was completely healed and never again had a problem with kidney or bladder infections.

These other healings we've experienced have been equally significant--perhaps even more so. I don't want to downplay Sara's physical healing, because it was a precious gift from God and showed His tremendous power. Still, the kids' other healings carry special significance because they affect eternity! Our precious children have begun to heal inwardly, though it's been a slow and painful process, and there is still a long way to go. None of us ever arrives, so we rejoice with every sign of progress and continue to pray when it seems like one step forward, two steps back.

Three-and-a-half years after the children came, when the adoption was at last final, we had a huge adoption party. People who hadn't seen Polly since the children first came to live with us could hardly believe their eyes! She was "little Miss Hostess with the Most-est." She'd ask people if they'd like more punch and bring it to them, ask how their children were doing, and generally carry on conversations with the crowd! What a change!

    The greatest growth came during her senior year of high school. Our training prepared us with the knowledge that during major milestones, the children would probably experience pain, missing their parents more than on average days. Sure enough, not only was Polly preparing to graduate, but she had also been nominated for homecoming queen, and she was deeply feeling the loss of her mother. To make matters more intense, at our school, the candidates for king and queen are required to share their testimonies in chapel in front of the entire student body and their teachers. Polly had *never* shared her life story-- especially not in public! She was in a stew and asked me several times if she had to tell everything about their family. I reassured her each time that it was totally up to her what she shared, but that what happened to her mother and the children was a major part of her life. *I* knew she would benefit from telling her story, but it had to come from her *own* willingness to open up.

    One night during this time period, I was checking on baby Anna, and Polly didn't realize I was up; I saw her come out of the bathroom, crying her eyes out. I quickly covered Anna with her blanket and followed Polly to her room, only to find her sitting on the floor of her walk-in closet, rocking back and forth, sobs wracking her tiny frame. I knelt beside her and held her, eventually asking her what was wrong. She croaked out, "I miss her so much!"

At that, both of us were reduced to sobs! We continued to hold each other and cry for a long time, and finally I told Polly that I knew I could never take the place of her mother, and I'd never try to, but that I was there for her. She smiled weakly and we pulled ourselves together, but it was a bonding time for us and a part of Polly's healing.

She asked me to help her with her homecoming speech, and she decided to include everything. She had me help her write out every word, knowing she'd be so nervous she could never share from an outline. The morning of chapel, she was a jittery heap, but Sara and I were there to support her, and we had the video camera rolling. She was amazing! It was extremely difficult for her, but she told everyone what had happened to her family. I don't think there was a dry eye--even the jocks were choked up! We were so proud of Polly! It was therapeutic for her to verbalize her pain, and we saw tremendous growth after that.

Soon after homecoming, the Hutchinson News did an article on our family, and it basically featured Polly with news of her homecoming crowning. The attention was good for her, and we've never quit thanking God for how He's working in her life. She's a hard worker and knows how to set and meet goals. Polly saved her money so she'd have a good-sized down payment for the car she bought after high school graduation. She worked at the Sunshine Home for about five years, first in the kitchen, then as a nurse aide and a med aide, and she continues to serve a temporary service as an aide. She took two years at Hutchinson Junior College, majoring in early childhood education. We are proud of her accomplishments and what a lovely young lady she is, inside and out.

Never one to be extremely demonstrative, it's been a challenge for Polly to live with me! I'm a real "huggy-kissy" person, and I need lots of physical and verbal input to be reassured of love. One day during Polly's first year at the junior college, I asked her if she even loved me. I was feeling insecure because she was busy and the family hardly had any time to see her, let alone share hearts! She mumbled out a "yes," in response, but I couldn't quit yet. I asked her *why* she loved me. She didn't want to answer, but I didn't turn away, waiting expectantly for a reply. Finally, she blurted out, "Because you're *there*!" Many times since then, as I did that day, I've grabbed her for a bear hug, quipping that she needs to hug me just because I'm "there!" She always grins her lopsided grin and endures the hug, putting one of her arms around me in a gesture of acceptance. Ahh, God's good!

Jeri has many gifts, and truly loves people with a giving heart, but she just seems to rub life the wrong way. Learning to cope with her way of dealing with pain was a long time coming for all of us. For example, it used to frustrate the entire family when Jeri would purposely irritate us, then turn right around and ask if she could get one of us a drink of water. We thought she was being a fake! After reading Gary Chapman's excellent book, *The Five Love Languages*, we realized that Jeri's primary love language was acts of service. Doing something nice for us was her way of letting us know that she really did care. Once we knew this, it was easier to receive love from Jeri, as well as give it to her in a way she would understand it.

Jeri does have a giving heart, and I'm convinced someday God will use that. She secretly gives money to those in need and has helped willingly when I've had a special project going. One of our favorite times together was spent scraping wallpaper all night a couple of years ago! She often offers to do things for others, and used to ask every few days to bake cookies for someone in need.

I'm always amazed that even when life has hit Jeri hard, she bounces back. There's a good side to her stubborn nature, causing her to never give up, no matter what. Although she hasn't been able to attach deeply with us, and it's been a challenge to remember this stems from her painful past, I try to realize it's not a personal rejection of me. It is hard to separate those feelings, though.

So many times, I've wanted to cry out, "Jeri, I'm sorry you lost your mother, but it's not my fault!

I'm the one who is here to help you! Please let me in!" But I've had to wait for her to be ready to accept me, with the realization that it may never happen to the degree I long for. I understand the feelings of loyalty that she has towards her birth family. I know that to her, loving us would seem like a betrayal to her family of origin--including her aunts and uncles. Still, she needs us, and I haven't given up on having the relationship the Lord wants for us.

Ashley is adapting beautifully to the life the Lord has provided for her. After weeks and months of near-perfect behavior, the first time she did anything wrong, I went into my bedroom and closed the door and shouted, "Yes!" Not that I wanted her to sin, but let's face it; everybody has a sin nature, and it's not normal for a six-year-old to be perfect. Obedience needs to be motivated by love, not fear of losing acceptance, and I'm much more confident that her desire to please me is more normal now that she's secure in her place with us. Her sweet spirit causes all those around her to want to pick her up and hold her! She's tender and fragile, but starting to show signs of resilience and strength as she grows in the Lord and makes her faith personal to her. We're thankful that she's secure enough to be herself.

Now that Ashley has entered the "turbulent teens"--which I say are *much* harder than the "terrible two's!"--she's facing some difficult issues from her past. She wonders why her birth dad doesn't write letters to her very often. She questions why the few letters she's received from him are mostly about Bible prophecy instead of personal interactions. She's uncomfortable with Eddie asking her to try to get me to let him call the children. She knows that part of the adoption agreement stated that the only contact between the children and their birth father was to be through letters until they're eighteen years old. She's starting to question why Polly has never gone to see him, since she's twenty years old, and that's making her face the unsettling idea that maybe she won't want to visit him, either. She longs to have the pictures and belongings of her birth mother so she can connect with her past in some way. She remembers her mother playing the guitar, singing "Puff the Magic Dragon" and "Amazing Grace," but grieves that most of her memories have faded away. She feels there is almost nothing left of her former life without those ties of having her mom's things.

Growth and healing are sometimes painful. You know what it's like when you've had a deep cut. At first you might not even feel the pain. After you see what happened, the message makes its way to your brain and you begin to experience the wound. You have to give it lots of care--cleansing and medicating and bandaging the tender place. When healing finally begins, the itch can be unnerving! Even after complete healing, there is still a scar.

That's how this has been for Ashley and Justin. They were tiny when their loss occurred, therefore much of it has only begun to sink in. Now that they can see what happened, the pain is making its way to their consciousness. That can seem scary, and it sure hurts a lot to take a hard look at the truth, but that's the only way to get to the healing. We've found an excellent Christian therapist who is staying in touch with us and making herself available to help these little ones find their way through their grief.

Healing is coming slowly, and I think that kind lasts longer. The healing our children have experienced so far is eternal, and I know the Lord isn't done with any of us yet. He will keep working and loving, patiently waiting for us to be ready to go deeper. We might just take baby steps at first, but as we step out, we go walking and leaping and praising God. *All the praise goes to Him!*

12. LOVER'S LEAP

This book would not be complete without discussing dating and the frequent resulting heartache. How well I remember my own broken heart during those sometimes turbulent times of seeking to find long-lasting love! Certainly, with five daughters and three sons, Tracy and I have our work cut out for us, trying to train them to view love and marriage in a way that is pleasing to God.

Not that Tracy and I are authorities, by any means! Neither of us had the kind of experience we hope and pray for our children. We desire purity for each of them, so we seek God's Word to try to gain understanding.

By the time Sara entered the teen years, we had already been letting her know for years that we preferred courtship over dating the way it's practiced in today's American society. Dating as we know it has proven itself to be a miserable failure, reflected by our high divorce rates. The happiness we thought we would gain by fulfilling our own desires has ended up causing untold grief to thousands of husbands and wives and their children.

Tracy and I don't feel that young men and women, hormones charged and ready to explode, have any business being alone together. We decided to approach the entire dating process as one in which we, as the parents, were in control.

Everyone says you learn how to parent your oldest child by making lots of mistakes, then hopefully the other children benefit from what you've learned! That was definitely the case with Sara. When she met a Christian young man during youth convention her junior year of high school, I was in favor of her spending time with him, since he "passed" our list of criteria: first and foremost, he shared her faith. He wasn't a Christian in name only, either, but was truly serious about his walk with God. He also lived in another town, which appealed to me, because I knew they wouldn't be able to spend all their free time together. Tracy and I determined that their outings would be chaperoned by one of us at all times. The boy was willing to abide by our guidelines, so I was able to welcome him.

The more time they spent with each other, the deeper Sara's feelings grew. This young man was her first love. As he prepared to leave for college and she began to face the reality of his pulling away, she held on tighter. She was shocked when he showed up at Christmas unexpectedly--with a fiancé! When his engagement was broken, Sara's hopes were sparked again, and all the more when he came home for the summer. They spent many happy hours together, and Sara was head over heels in love with him.

Determined to show him she was right for him, Sara followed him to the university that fall, but he wasn't interested in the kind of commitment Sara desired from him.

Unfortunately, since we had seldom let Sara be alone with a young man, her experience at college proved to be less than desirable. Tracy and I didn't realize that we hadn't prepared her for all the freedom she would encounter at the university. Although it was a Christian campus, she worked off-campus and quickly fell in with the wrong crowd, making poor choices with her new-found freedom. Her straying was intricately designed to get her first love's attention. She hoped he would see her pain and rush to her side, but he didn't respond by rescuing her.

Sara ended up withdrawing from the university, returning as a broken young lady. She came home for a short time, then moved in with two girlfriends. When another school year rolled around, she enrolled in another Christian college, but once again, her choices led her down a destructive path. Still searching to fill her inner void, she was soon engaged to a young man who turned out to be a compulsive liar. What was worse, we were fearful for her life because the fellow was so unstable. She withdrew from college again and came back home, this time more ready to discover what had caused her to stray from the teachings she'd received as a child.

Tracy and I grieved over the part we played in Sara's floundering. Hindsight is revealing, and looking back, we can see that we were too strict with Sara if we planned to let her go away to school. Not only did we restrict her involvement with boys, but she really wasn't allowed to do much of anything, even with girlfriends or in a crowd. She was seldom in a position to make choices about her actions, because we controlled her at almost every opportunity.

By now you might be noticing my use of the word "control." I've had to face the fact that I'm an extremely controlling person, one of the characteristics common to adult children of alcoholics. Since our childhoods were out of control, we like to feel we have some control in life now. How hard it has been for me to realize that I can't control my children indefinitely; I must let go of them and trust the Lord, Who loves them even more than I do. The goal is to train the children so that by the time they leave home, they know how to exercise self-control, being led by the Holy Spirit. This cannot happen if they're never given situations to make some decisions on their own. The best scenario is to gradually let them have more privileges while they're still at home. Then if they fall, we parents are still there to help them up and teach them and comfort them, much as we did when they took a tumble while learning to walk.

Part of the pressure Sara experienced stems from the feeling that in order to be accepted and "cool," one must have "somebody"--even elementary students are expected to have boyfriends and girlfriends. Our little Ashley began receiving Valentine's Day gifts in second grade--not something that thrilled me! Saying you love somebody without making a commitment to that person is just practicing for divorce, so we don't like our children to begin expressing their feelings until they're old enough to do something long-term about them!

Even with the mistakes we made with Sara, she had a foundation and a true love for the Lord. She was restored to Him and we began to pray with her for an office job so she could attend church regularly and hopefully avoid the pitfalls of working with a partying crowd in a restaurant.

After applying at several offices that first week, Sara was surprised to receive a call from Steve Graber on Friday, since she hadn't even applied there. He wanted to know if she might be interested in working for him. Steve is an attorney in Hutchinson and a godly man who is strong in Christ. Sara excitedly interviewed for the position, but didn't go on false pretenses. She was honest with Steve about her struggles, but he showed her the love and grace of Christ and hired her. She's been working in his office for over a year and a half, and under the ministry of Steve and his wife, Melanie, Sara has had her identity in Christ firmly established. She's working on her para-legal degree in the evenings and loves being in an office where Jesus Christ is glorified!

As she began to heal under the Graber's precious ministry, Sara quit searching to fill her emptiness with another relationship. God was teaching her that *He* wanted to be her first love, and He was the only One Who would return her love completely--giving even *more* than she could give.

    Years ago, when Sara was in eighth grade, we took a missions trip to inner-city Chicago, sponsored by Central Christian School. At the last minute, one young man contracted chicken pox and was unable to go, so Danny Nowlan went in his place. He and Sara were best friends, and we were glad to let her sit with him on the plane coming home.

    Little did we know that he viewed Sara as more than a friend! She later told me that he had leaned over and kissed her--right there on the plane with us a few rows ahead of them! She was the first girl he'd ever kissed! She didn't encourage a repeat performance, and they went on being good friends until he transferred to another school in ninth grade. The lack of contact didn't change the fact that the seeds of love were present way back then!

    Danny's mother and I talked with each other occasionally, and the two young people ran into each other now and then, but it wasn't until she had returned home from the second college that they really began to visit back and forth. In fact, we had decided to go shopping during Christmas break, and Sara really didn't want to go along. I encouraged her to come since it was a family time of sharing, so she grudgingly complied. We ran into Danny that day and the two of them began to call each other. One thing led to another, and soon they were dating seriously.

    While we're on the subject, so often our kids from small communities or Christian schools think there aren't very many members of the opposite sex to "pick from." They feel life is passing them by and they are pressured to leave home to find somebody. I hold to the truth that if young people will lovingly submit to their parents and seek God's plan for them, He will lead them to someone who is "right." In obeying and honoring her parents, Sara was in the right place at the right time to see Danny again!

Having learned a little from our previous misjudgments, Tracy and I decided to give the kids more freedom. Still, we wanted to be sure Danny understood our expectations, and he graciously endured "the talk," where we outlined our hopes and desires and requests as they entered this new phase of their relationship, moving from being good friends to testing the waters of romantic love. Danny was just precious, willing to abide by our guidelines of not spending lots of time alone, rather trying to do things with family or groups of friends.

Watching their love grow over the past few months has been a delight, and we thank God for pairing them up. Sara says that only as she was willing to quit looking for love was God truly able to bless her. The principle of giving up and letting go is so important to receiving God's best! We've seen so many young people miss God's blessing because they insisted on taking love at an early age instead of waiting on the Lord. Sara and Danny will be married June 12th, 1999, and we know they've both received a real treasure in each other.

Polly took a long time to entertain the idea of dating anybody. One boy, who dared to talk to her in seventh grade, was rewarded with a kick in the shins! She made it known early on that she wasn't interested in boys, and it took a couple of years of high school to change her mind. Finally, one young man convinced her to attend homecoming with him. They became a kind of "couple," having an unspoken arrangement that a few days before homecoming or Junior/Senior Banquet, he'd ask her to go with him and she'd agree. This went on for two-and-a-half years. They were always chaperoned and they never had any other dates except for sitting together when the class went out for pizza or sometimes at ball games.

This was all fine, except that their senior year, days before Junior/Senior Banquet, the young man still hadn't asked Polly to go. She'd had her dress for weeks, and was excited about the event, but still wasn't worried about his silence, because he *always* asked at the last minute. Well, three days before the big day, he left her a note saying he wasn't going to take her. She found out he'd planned to ask somebody else, a girl who didn't attend their school. Polly was crushed! Not only was she hurt that he hadn't had any more consideration than that--nobody else would ask her, being sure the other fellow would, like always-- but now she was faced with attending the banquet alone, and her senior year, no less!

Polly and I talked for quite awhile, trying to think of the best solution. Finally, I convinced her to call a friend from church to see if he'd go with her. This went completely against my usual advice: I don't like for girls to call boys or ask them out under normal circumstances! This boy had always been friendly towards Polly from a distance (she never let anybody get closer than that!), and he immediately agreed to go. I think they had a lovely time, and even though I felt for the other boy, I still found it ironic that he ended up at the banquet alone!

Polly has been dating a very nice young man who loves to farm. Josh has spent some pleasant times at our house, and we think he's pretty special. He has a way of connecting with Polly's soul in such a way that she feels safe enough to reveal the loveliness our family has come to cherish, and she's learning to trust.

Nathan has always been the kind of boy the girls can really be friends with. We've had many talks with him to be sure he understands the principle that the young man, training to lead his home, must take the leadership role in relationships. We don't ever want a young lady to have to tell Nathan things have gone far enough; we want *him* to keep things under control in every aspect of his dating life. Our resolve to "let go" is being tested with Nathan! We're learning to truly trust the Lord as we allow Nathan to make more decisions about girls. It's a good feeling to have my 17 year old son share his heart with me; he's seeking the Lord and I can see Nathan growing before my very eyes.

We want our kids' friends to feel welcome in

our home. Doing things in a group makes for healthier relationships. The pressure is off when they can just "hang" with a group instead of feeling like they need to impress one special person.

We hope that as the other children begin to show an interest in spending time with members of the opposite sex, we'll have found a good balance. We want to protect them *and* prepare them, which can make for an interesting combination!

Passion is a powerful force. I heard one speaker liken it to a train. It might take awhile to get going, but once you've reached a certain speed, even if you want to stop, it takes some time to put on the brakes--and you might not be able to do so quickly enough. So many Christian young people have good intentions and don't plan to take things too far, but once they've begun to experiment, it can be too difficult to stop soon enough.

The selfish, sin nature says, "I must have you now or the opportunity will be lost!" The Holy Spirit-controlled nature says, "I can wait on the Lord. If you are right for me, you will still be right for me in a few months, or even years." We encourage our children to give love time so it's true nature can be revealed.

I look at my children and their "love lives" and go back in time over twenty-three years to the beginning of my relationship with Tracy. My dad had never liked the boys I liked, and vice versa! If I liked a guy, Dad couldn't stand him, but the fellas he liked were the type to attack me as soon as we were alone!

(See why I don't think girls and boys should be alone?!)

Well, the whole story about Tracy and I meeting and his marriage proposal is another book, but suffice it to say that when I took Tracy home to meet my parents, he and Daddy hit it off just fine. They shared their testimonies in the backyard all afternoon, and I was becoming more confident that Tracy was a good choice; after all, he was the first and only guy that both Daddy and I liked!

Twenty-three years ago, when I first met Tracy, love seemed like a distant dream, always out of reach. There were many painful moments as we learned to love unconditionally. Real love isn't based on what we get out of it, but rather what we can give. Only through a commitment to go through life's mountains and valleys together do we find a love that is secure. No need for lover's leap there!

13. WALKING AND LEAPING AND CARRYING THE TORCH!

Soon after Anna was born in the spring of 1996, I learned that I'd been selected for a special honor: I was one of a group of people who had been chosen to carry the Olympic torch through Wichita, Kansas. A dear friend, Rob Mackey, had nominated me by submitting my name and an essay about me. He'd written about our adoption, and I was honored that he'd gone to the trouble to enter my name. I thought that he and his wife Shirley deserved the honor--they are some of the finest folks around, having gracefully overcome great trials in their own lives! At any rate, I was one of the people chosen, so I needed to hurry and prepare for the event.

Now, you need to understand that even under the best of circumstances, I'm not especially athletic! Let's just say that a few years ago when my brother Bob overheard someone at church asking if I'd like to be on the softball team, we had to help him up off the floor before his laughing sent him to the hospital! I consider lifting tortilla chips to my mouth exercise!

I've been blessed with a slightly above average metabolism that served me well for over three decades, so I've gotten by with very little exercise until recent years. That suited me just fine, because the only exercise I really enjoy is swimming.

Unfortunately, there wasn't a category for that in this Olympic precursor! To make matters worse, I was to run two-and-a-half months after giving birth! Not only was I out of shape, but I also still weighed about twenty pounds more than normal! Add to this the fact that the Olympics provided our running outfits--not flattering in the least!

    The people in charge of the torch-carrying assured me that I didn't have to run the entire distance, so I settled for a modified jog, walk, jog, walk. I thought all was okay until Channel 3 News contacted me about running a clip on me and my family! I believed people would be touched and possibly motivated to consider adoption, so I agreed. I had to face the fact that I would have my ridiculous attempt at something physical broadcast all over Kansas! It turned out to be lots of fun, and Sara and Anna even got to be on television. In the background, we could hear Sara calling, "I love you, Mom!" before I took off running (okay, jogging, walking, jogging, walking!). Those words are still a torch all their own, lighting a path through the darkness of this world and spurring me on in this journey of motherhood! "I love you, too, Sara, and all you kids!"

    When we first got the children, Tracy and I were almost amused as people would stop us to say how much they admired us and what wonderful people we were. We tried to find the words to explain that we weren't really wonderful; we're just willing and obedient! There are many other people who could do a better job than we have done with the children, and certainly others who could afford a family of this size better than we've been able to. Still, the Lord has chosen to use us, and we're the benefactors of that plan, growing in ways we had never dreamed possible. God has shown us many selfish areas of our hearts, and He patiently continues to change us and use us, in spite of ourselves.

Still, we needed to learn to deal with the attention people insisted upon giving us. One special lesson came to me when I was chosen by Sterling College, in Sterling, Kansas, to receive the Alumni of the Year Award in May of 1997. Word of our adoption had reached the "powers that be," and they interviewed me and asked that I not only give an acceptance speech, but also share some of my original music at the alumni banquet honoring myself and two other individuals receiving other awards.

I wasn't sure what to say! Like others receiving an award, I wanted to give the Lord credit for what He'd done in my life and the children's. I started planning to say the usual thing--"It's nothing, really. Only the Lord has done this...." Suddenly, I stopped in my thoughts! If the Lord had done it, it wasn't "nothing"! He began to show me a wonderful truth. Yes, it was His doing, so I wasn't to have false humility and act like it was nothing!

By the time I gave my speech, I was pumped! I shared that according to statistics, I should have been an alcoholic. I should have been divorced. I probably would have been dead! Instead, by God's grace, I was fulfilling His call on my life! I'm the faithful wife of my husband and loving mother of eight children! The Lord has done marvelous things in our lives and I'll be the first one to stand and applaud Him, the King of kings and Lord of lords, Who cares about every detail of our lives and involves Himself intimately with us! Yes, I accepted the award on His behalf, and I'll lovingly, joyfully, and gratefully cast it at His feet in glory, for He is worthy!

Meanwhile, He is teaching us to carry the torch that really matters--the light of His love!

14. LEAPING THROUGH HOOPS

I've always thought those little dogs that leap through hoops are hilarious--sort of nervous little guys in their out-of-place outfits and surroundings. I am sure that none of my dogs, past or future, could ever have the necessary discipline required to learn the tricks these entertaining canines can perform!

Still, I find *myself* identifying with them! I make a running leap at my goals, setting each one higher than the last one. I run circles around myself, chasing my tail and striving to make an impression on an undefined crowd of spectators.

Coming from an undisciplined past, once I became a disciple of Jesus (which means *disciplined follower*), and He began to change me, I felt justified--and even superior--as I outdid myself. I can now admit that I'm a perfectionist, and I've finally realized that's nothing to brag about! Perfection is a lofty goal always out of reach, so those of us trying to capture it become driven.

Only after my father died did I really begin to realize how much of what I did was designed to gain his approval--everything from the way I cooked and cleaned house to the effectiveness of my ministry. One of the most special memories I have with Daddy took place just a few months before he died. As we sat in his living room, he looked across the room at me and said he knew he hadn't said it enough, but he was proud of me. At first, I wanted to say, "I know, Daddy; you don't have to say it." But the truth was, I needed to hear it and he needed to express it. It did wonders for me, literally lifting a burden from my shoulders as he affirmed me with his accepting words Still, I find myself driven too often to perform, and even now that he's gone, I try to live up to what I think would have gained his approval.

My obsessive nature showed up the most in my house-keeping years ago. Everything had a place, and my day wasn't complete unless I'd finished all the household tasks. I'd even make the family late to church so I could finish washing every last breakfast dish. (Okay, my perfectionism didn't extend to being punctual!) My house was never *Better Homes and Gardens* quality, mind you, but I liked it to be neat and clean.

I also strove for perfection when I returned to college as an adult. I had a 4.0 until my last year, when I got one B. I strove to perform, thankful that Tracy was willing to help get the children bathed and put to bed so I could study. He also scrubbed the bathrooms and mopped the floors every week. I achieved the honor of being named a Kelsey scholar and graduated Magna Cum Laude. Once again, I thought it was all for the Lord, so He'd get glory for what He had done in me. I felt I must prove that since the Lord was in my life, I could do my best and live up to my potential--so everything else suffered while I performed.

By the time our adopted children came to live with us, I had eased up, and when they arrived, I had to "chill out" even *more*. I think that's one reason God gave me so many children--so I would be faced with a challenge that was bigger than me. It caused me to re-evaluate my priorities and depend on Him more. The dirty socks dropped on the floor on the way to the hamper still stress me, and I prefer a semblance of order, but I've learned to chuckle at our messy lives and make the best of the situation. Instead of making my family miserable, I can usually put off deep-cleaning until the weekend, and if we don't get to it then, it will still be waiting for us when we find time. I understand that people are more important than surroundings, and as long as I don't enter the boys' rooms, I can deal with the rest of the house.

One thing that I will *never* understand, though, is why nobody else can ever learn the basic skills necessary to change the toilet paper roll. I'm about as mechanically inclined as a tadpole, yet I'm the only one who seems to be capable of maneuvering the delicate task of removing the empty roll and replacing it with a full one. It doesn't just happen at home, either; at the craft mall, at church, at friends' houses, and even at Wal-Mart, it seems the person who has been in the restroom before me has invariably used the last of the roll, and doesn't possess the ability to change it! Some people fight about whether it should roll over or under, and great debates have ensued over that question, causing even Ann Landers to falter a bit in her advice, but at my house, it's never a worry. Since I'm the only one who changes the thing, I can have it the way I want. Not that it matters that much to me--I would just be happy if I could count on there always being some toilet paper *available* when needed!

Now you're seeing my perfectionist side, the part of me that can be hard to live with. The fact remains that part of me would still like to live in a fantasy world! I like it there--a place where there is order and peace and happiness at all times! I get frustrated trying to be the virtuous woman we read about in Proverbs 31. Here's her profile:

> She's energetic, burning the candle at both ends.
> She sews, does crafts, cooks gourmet meals, and loves to cook--even early in the morning.
> She's a nutritionist, knowing breakfast is important to the best function of her household.
> She knows how to delegate and manage--she's organized and prepared.
> She's a successful business woman.
> She's a teacher.
> She looks elegant, doesn't neglect her appearance, and has an inner dignity that shines. (No, she's not the Enjoli woman! Remember her commercial? She could "bring home the bacon, fry it up in a pan,

and never, never let him forget he's a man. . . .")

No, this woman fears the Lord.

Even with her busy schedule, she takes in and helps the poor and needy of her community--she doesn't just send a check.

Her children think she's wonderful (mine would, too, if I had breakfast ready every morning and servants to help with the chores! My definition of a hot breakfast is a pop tart fresh from the toaster!).

No, my life no longer even vaguely resembles hers. A typical morning at my house reveals the trash running over, someone with a curling iron burn, the egg casserole I've tried desperately to provide for my family not being done in time for them to eat it before they make their mad dash out the door, someone unable to find his shoes, and the necessary sack lunch left behind--AUGHHHH!

Even Thanksgiving morning last year, Anna managed to paint her own fingernails up to her wrists and call 9-1-1, sending a police officer to our front porch as guests arrived! When I get on the phone, it's even worse: one morning recently she managed to spill baby powder all over the bathroom mat, eat cold macaroni and distribute it evenly across the entire first floor, and smash eight raw eggs onto the kitchen floor, all in the time frame of one call!

I used to picture us as the family on the "Sound of Music," me with my guitar and little charges following behind in coordinating outfits, singing through the countryside and shivering together during storms, a song always ready to chase away our blues. No more Von Trapp Family Syndrome remains now, though! Our lives are so far from perfect!

All those Von Trapp family children needed in the movie was Maria. They wanted her, grieved her when she was gone, and accepted her with open arms when she returned to them. That's not how it is at my house.

Jeri ran away from home last October. She was in a youth detention center/shelter first, then a foster home for about four months. The foster parents asked the case worker to find another home for Jeri, because she was unwilling to live by their house rules, and she was even kicked out of school. She ended up back at the youth center, finally being released from SRS custody because she turned eighteen May 8, 1999; social services had no alternate placement for her. She has alienated so many of her family members who love her; everyone hurts to see her making such poor choices, including running with a rough crowd of kids. She's lashed out at those who really care for her, making false accusations, thinking she'll feel better by hurting those she's rejected. If she can blame others and make them appear guilty, then she feels justified in rebelling.

Jeri is trying to fill her inner void with people

who are only using her. She has lived for her eighteenth birthday, planning to visit her father in prison, hoping to connect with her past and find her identity again. The big day has come and gone, but she hasn't gone to see Eddie yet. I think there is some fear that reality won't match up to her dreams. Jeri makes me think of Annie in the orphanage--hoping against hope that her parents will come and claim her. Of course, in Jeri's case that isn't possible, but there's that part in her heart that is still the ten year old little girl who fantasizes that all of this has been a dream and her folks will show up and make things like they used to be.

It's been a heart-wrenching time for us, a time of re-evaluating our parenting, our choices, our faith. My heart breaks for Jeri. I've gone through the questions of what I could have done differently to better meet her needs. I've looked for where to place the blame. The truth is, though, it's not usually tied up so neatly.

Shadrack, Meshack, and Abedneggo were the Hebrew young men who were told that if they didn't bow down to worship the ruler, they would be thrown into the fire to be burned to death. The fire was heated up seven times hotter than normal. These guys wouldn't bow down; they were determined to worship God and Him alone, even if it meant death.

I love what they said right before they were thrown into the fiery furnace. They declared that God was well able to save them! But if not...! Even if the Lord didn't save them from the flames, they were still going to worship Him! I wish we didn't have to go through this trial with Jeri. God is well able to change the circumstances. But if not... we will still trust Him. He is worth our devotion, our worship, and our obedience, even when things don't go the way we hoped or planned!

    I can never be good enough for Jeri. I've tried. I've cried. I've prayed. Still, I haven't been able to reach her. I've wanted to make her see that love isn't a mushy feeling; it's an action--something we do. It's being there for somebody on days when it feels good to be there and on those days when it isn't so easy. It's sticking with it, trying to do what's best for that person instead of what is comfortable. It's being there today and the next day and the next one, too. I'll be there for her, even in the tomorrows that stretch ahead. Even when she doesn't want me. I'll still be here waiting, because that's what love does. There's no animosity towards her. Years ago, I heard an evangelist say, "Hurt people, hurt people," and I know that all the anger coming out of Jeri in such harmful ways is only a symptom of the deep pain she's experienced in her short life.

    Sometimes I wonder if even the Lord can be enough for Jeri's needs--only because she holds him afar. He promised to be a Father to the fatherless. Does that mean that in the areas where parents haven't been enough, He will fill those places, too? Every child, even if he's eighty years old, has a place inside that *only* the Lord can fill. Jeri's pain runs deep, but I'm convinced there is no place too deep for His love to fill. If only she'll let Him in!

Meanwhile, I face what feels like a major failure. Just when it begins to overwhelm me, and I strive to find a way to fix everything, I remember the words of a dear sister in Christ. Miss Debbye Simpson, from Sterling, Kansas, used to encourage me with these words, and they still come back to me today. She would say to me during times of discouragement, "Sister Spencer, God did not call you to succeed. He called you to be faithful!" And when I'm overwhelmed, thinking, "I can't do this," I calm down, realizing that's right where I need to be, so the Lord can work. I used to seem so capable, but now, especially with the fibromyalgia, I must rely on the Lord for each day. Slowly, I'm learning that's a good thing.

During one particularly painful time of rehashing how I'd failed Sara, the Lord got my attention. He reminded me that He is perfect in every way, including being a perfect Father. He created two children, Adam and Eve, with every good thing. They had every opportunity available to them to do right. Still, *they chose to sin!* I still get comfort from knowing that if *His* children rebelled, even with Him as their *perfect* Father, then perhaps I shouldn't take it too personally when my children also rebel, since I'm *not* perfect!

I had to take an honest look at *why* I want my

children to be perfect, too. Naturally, I want them to be spared a life of sin, but a major factor is also that I see their behavior as a reflection of *me*. I've had to die to that part of me, realizing parenting is about *them*, not me. Our children have a sin nature and they must find their own way to the cross, learning what grace really means as they apply their knowledge of God's love and forgiveness to their own sinful condition.

I'd *rather* be perfect. But I'm not on this earth to impress anybody. I'm an earthen vessel, imperfect, yet willing. Others' opinions of me are not the measuring stick--not even Jeri's. Not even mine. I can't perform for anybody--no tricks, no leaping through hoops. Just obedience... just as I am. And hopefully the joy of hearing my Heavenly Father say, "Well done, thou good and *faithful* servant... enter thou into the joy of thy lord." (Matthew 25:21, italics mine)

15. TO THE "LEAPS" OF THESE

Okay, I've taken a little poetic liberty with the verse from Matthew 25--the one that says whatever we've done to the least of these, we've actually done to the Lord. I just thought this title fit my book better!

In all seriousness, though, I've had to realize that everything I've done, whether good and loving, or bad and selfish, has actually been directed towards my Lord. I can't say I love Him, Whom I've never seen, and then not practically show love to the people He has put into my life. It's a sobering thought to realize that how we treat others reflects our true feelings for Him!

He has uncovered so many areas of selfishness in me. I love solitude and need it occasionally, and at times I've found the chaos and noise at home an almost unbearable intrusion on my sanity! My creative juices dry up under such racket! Writing a song, though, isn't as important as drying a tear or reading a story with a little one in my lap--and to be honest, not many of my eight will tolerate such behavior anymore! They're growing up *so* quickly!

I must ask myself: would I consider Jesus to be an intrusion on my busy schedule or creativity?

People have asked us if we'd do it again, taking the children knowing what we know now about what it has required of us. Yes! We would do some things differently, such as joining an adoption support group and getting counseling for our entire family to help with our many adjustments, but there's no way to turn back the pages of time. Our lives are not "neat" anymore. We've said goodbye to Ward and June Cleaver, goodbye to structure, but hello to Jesus in new ways. We've lost our identity of who we were before, but we've gained so much more. We *love* the children God has placed in our lives. We love the new way He leads us and cares for us as we realize that we can't parent without Him. We admit that all we can do is provide a place for the children, doing our best, but trusting Him to do what we can't do--those unseen, eternal things of the heart.

As we call out on God, admitting our deep need for Him, He's there on the spot! We didn't experience Him as deeply when our lives were so picture perfect! Every trial, every pain, every challenge is welcome again and again as we experience Jesus in our midst in new ways!

Each of us--all who are "sheep," anyway--has a responsibility to find where we fit in the sheep's activities. It is possible to do good without being a "sheep," because being a true "sheep" means having accepted Jesus Christ as Savior. It means realizing we fall short of God's perfect ways, and we know we need Him in our lives to bring forgiveness and cleansing. According to the verses in Matthew, though, it isn't a good idea to be a sheep without doing good!

Perhaps your heart has always been touched when hearing of the starving people in India, or you might get choked up thinking of the homeless in your city. They are everywhere, you know. Maybe tears come to your eyes when you think of the sick and dying lying in hospital beds or nursing homes. It could be that you have a heart for prisoners who might not have ever heard the Good News that Someone loves them and wants to give them *real* freedom. Or perhaps, like Tracy and me, it's the little strangers who tug at your heart.

Whatever it is, know that the area that touches you is probably the area where God is calling you to make a difference.

The Lord has told people to do some pretty crazy things. He told Noah to build an ark even though it had never rained before. He asked Joseph to go ahead and be wedded to Mary, even though she was pregnant and the child didn't belong to Joseph. He asked a couple of unqualified, ignorant followers of His in the middle of Kansas to open their home to four children, even though the only thing they had going for them was their willingness to obey.

Jesus tells us that when we give, we actually receive, and dying to ourselves is the way to life. Often His ways seem backwards to our way of thinking. He is the One Who sees the big picture, though, and He knows how to accomplish eternal results.

We read in James that pure and undefiled

religion is to care for the widows and orphans (1:27). He also encourages us to show our faith by the way we live, not just by our verbal claims (2:18).

After reading our story, you know I'm not saying that it's always easy to live out our faith. But the Lord wants us to move out of our comfort zones. He's literally *waiting* for us to feed Him, give Him drink, invite Him in, clothe Him, or visit Him. *That's* where the real life begins. *That's* where we're stripped of self and we begin to see that He not only *receives* the ministry we're willing to be a part of; He also actually *performs* it through us. We get to know Him in a new way as we are changed and eternity is affected in our small corner of the world, and in the "leaps" of these.

Go ahead--take the leap! And may God richly bless you as you serve Jesus. Amen!

BOOKING INFORMATION

Becky is available as a speaker, enjoying sharing her adventure in adoption and how to find your life calling, as well as teaching women to love their husbands. (Yes, it can be taught!) Many women who had given up hope for their marriages have been encouraged and challenged through her ministry. Consider having her come to share at your:

        church
        mother/daughter banquet
        retreat
        ladies' organization
        civic event

She is also available to do weddings, county or state fairs, and share her original music in concert. Her recording, "Tears of a Clown," with 10 original songs, is available in cassette ($11.67) and c.d. ($17.50). Price includes tax and shipping and handling. Send check or money order with your name and address to:

        Becky Yates Spencer
        406 West Avenue A
        Buhler, KS 67522
        316-543-6518

Most importantly, if you want to know more about what it means to know and serve Jesus Christ, please write! Becky would be honored to respond!